COOKSHELF

Low Fat

Kathryn Hawkins

DP
DEMPSEY PARR

First published in Great Britain in 1998 by
Dempsey Parr
13 Whiteladies Road
Clifton
Bristol BS8 1PB

ISBN: 1-84084-288-1

Produced by Haldane Mason, London

Acknowledgements
Art Director: Ron Samuels
Editorial Director: Sydney Francis
Managing Editor: Jo-Anne Cox
Design: dap ltd
Photography: Iain Bagwell
Home Economist: Kathryn Hawkins
Nutritional information: Anne Sheasby and Annette Yates

Colour Reproduction by
Inka Graphics, Cardiff

Printed in China

Note

Cup measurements in this book are for American cups. Tablespoons are assumed to be 15 ml. Unless otherwise stated, milk is assumed to be full fat, eggs are medium and pepper is freshly ground black pepper. The calorie counts and fat content analysis do not include the serving suggestions.

Contents

Introduction

No one who has more than a passing interest in their health can be unaware of the problems associated with a diet that contains too much fat. A high level of fat consumption is implicated in obesity – and all that that entails – coronary disease, diabetes and even cancer. The message that we should all cut down on the fat in our diets is reinforced every time we go shopping, and it is almost impossible to walk around a supermarket without being beset on all sides by labels proclaiming low-fat this, reduced-fat that and no-fat the other.

Cutting the amount of fat in our diets is, of course, an effective way to lose weight, simply because it will reduce the number of calories we consume, as well as reducing the likelihood that we will contract a serious disease. However, before we cut fat out of our lives completely, it is important to remember that we all need to include a certain amount of fat in our daily intake of food if our bodies are to function properly. Essential fatty acids are needed to build cell membranes and for other vital bodily functions. Our brain tissue, nerve sheaths and bone marrow need fat, for example, and we all need fat to protect vital organs such as our liver, kidneys and heart.

Nutritionists suggest that we should aim to cut our intake of fat to 27-30 per cent of our total daily calorie intake. If your average diet totals 2000 calories, this will mean eating no more than about 75 g/2¾ oz of fat a day. As a guide, bear in mind that most people consume about 40 per cent of their daily calories in the form of fat. Remember, however, that if you are being treated for any medical condition, you must discuss with your family doctor the changes you propose making in your diet before you begin your new regime.

When you are thinking about reducing your intake of fat, it is important to know that fats can be broadly divided into saturated and unsaturated fat. Saturated fats are those that are solid at room temperature, and they are found mainly in animal products – butter and cheese, high-fat meats (sausages, pâté, streaky bacon), cakes, chocolate, potato crisps, biscuits, coconut and hydrogenated (hardened) vegetable or fish oils. Unsaturated fats are healthier – but they are still fats. Your target should be a reduction to 8 per cent of your daily calories in the form of saturated fats, with the remainder in the form of unsaturated fats. These are usually liquid at room temperature and come from vegetable sources – olive oil, ground nut oil, sunflower oil, safflower oil and corn oil. Remember, though, that oil is only another name for liquid fat. Using oil instead of margarine or butter to fry onions or garlic will do nothing to reduce your overall intake of fat.

INGREDIENTS

One of the simplest and most beneficial changes you can make in your diet is to change from full-fat milk, cream, cheese and yogurt to a low- or reduced-fat equivalent. Semi-skimmed milk, for example, has all the nutritional benefits of whole milk but 10 g/⅓ oz of fat per pint compared with 23 g/¾ oz of fat per pint in whole milk. Use skimmed milk to make custards and sauces and you will not notice the difference in flavour. Low-fat yogurt or fromage frais mixed with chopped chives is a delicious and healthy alternative to butter or sour cream.

Most vegetables are naturally low in fat and can be used to make a meal of meat or fish go further. Recent nutritional research indicates that we should all aim to eat five portions of fresh fruit and vegetables every day because they contain what are known as antioxidant vitamins, including beta carotene (which creates vitamin A in the body) and vitamins C and E. The antioxidant vitamins in vegetables are thought to help prevent a number of degenerative illnesses (including cancer, heart disease, arthritis and even ageing of the skin) and to protect the body from the harmful effects of pollution and ultraviolet light, which can damage the body's cells. Phytochemicals, which occur naturally in plants, are thought to be instrumental in the fight against cancer.

Steaming is the best way to cook vegetables to preserve their goodness. Boiling can, for example, destroy up to three-quarters of the vitamin C present in green vegetables. If you have to boil, cook the vegetables as quickly as possible and avoid over-cooking, which also destroys the carotene.

If you have time, it is a good idea to make your own stock to use as the basis of casseroles and soups. The ready-made stocks and stock cubes that are available from shops are often high in salt and artificial flavourings. Instead, use fresh herbs and spices in the water in which vegetables have been cooked or in which dried mushrooms have been soaked. Liquids in which meat and fish of various kinds have been cooked should be saved, too. Chill the liquid in the refrigerator and you will easily be able to remove and discard the fat, which will have risen to the top of the container and solidified.

Pasta, noodles, pulses and grains can all be used in the low-fat diet, and they are useful for bulking out dishes. Pasta is available in a wide range of shapes, and it is excellent for boosting your carbohydrate intake. Inadequate intake of carbohydrate can result in fatigue and poor energy levels. Wholemeal (whole wheat) pasta is also particularly high in fibre, which helps to speed the passage of waste material through the digestive system. Stir cooked brown rice into soups and casseroles to thicken them, or mix one part red lentils with three parts lean minced (ground) beef to make a smaller amount of meat go further. Before you buy, check that noodles and pasta have not been enriched with egg. Look out instead for wholemeal (whole wheat) or rice varieties.

EQUIPMENT

Good quality non-stick pans and cookware will directly reduce the amount of fat needed for cooking, and are easier to clean. Use plastic implements or wooden spoons with non-stick pans so that you do not scratch the surface.

A ridged frying pan (skillet) makes it possible to cook with the minimum amount of fat or oil, because the fat drips down between the ridges rather than being absorbed by the food.

When you are stir-frying, use a small amount of oil. Keep the heat constant and the food moving to ensure quick, even cooking. Use a non-stick wok, which will help you cut down still further on the amount of oil you need.

Use a perforated spoon to remove food from the frying pan (skillet), so that cooking juices are left behind. Absorbent kitchen paper is useful both for draining surface oil and fat from food that has just been cooked, but it can also be used to mop up fat that rises to the top during cooking. Use plain, unpatterned paper so that no dye is transferred to the food.

Soups & Starters

Many favourite snacks and starters – especially those that we buy ready-prepared on supermarket shelves and in cans – are surprisingly high in fat. Next time, before you buy, think instead about making some of the appetizing recipes on the following pages – they will get your meal off to a wonderful low-fat start.

Soups are a traditional first course, but, served with crusty bread, they can also be a satisfying meal in their own right. Although it does take a little longer, consider making your own stock by using the liquid left after cooking vegetables and the juices from fish and meat that have been used as the base of casseroles. Use a potato to thicken your soups rather than stirring in the traditional thickener of flour and water – or, worse, flour and fat.

If you want a change from soup, try a few starters such as a light Cheesy Ham and Celery Savoury or Parsleyed Chicken and Ham Pâté served with a refreshing salad and crisp-breads or flavour-filled Spinach Cheese Moulds (Molds).

Chicken & Asparagus Soup

Serves 4 • Calories per serving: 236 • Fat content per serving: 2.9 g

INGREDIENTS

225 g/8 oz fresh asparagus
850 ml/1 1/2 pints/3 3/4 cups fresh chicken stock
150 ml/5 fl oz/2/3 cup dry white wine
1 sprig each fresh parsley, dill and tarragon
1 garlic clove
60 g/2 oz/1/3 cup vermicelli rice noodles
350 g/12 oz lean cooked chicken, finely shredded
salt and white pepper
1 small leek

1 Wash the asparagus and trim away the woody ends. Cut each spear into pieces 4 cm/1½ inches long.

2 Pour the stock and wine into a large saucepan and bring to the boil.

3 Wash the herbs and tie them with clean string. Peel the garlic clove and add, with the herbs, to the saucepan together with the asparagus and noodles. Cover and simmer for 5 minutes.

4 Stir in the chicken and plenty of seasoning. Simmer gently for a further 3-4 minutes or until heated through.

5 Trim the leek, slice it down the centre and wash under running water to remove any dirt. Shake dry and shred finely.

6 Remove the herbs and garlic and discard.

7 Ladle the soup into warm bowls, sprinkle with shredded leek and serve at once.

VARIATION

You can use any of your favourite herbs in this recipe, but choose those with a subtle flavour so that they do not overpower the asparagus. Small, tender asparagus spears give the best results and flavour.

COOK'S TIP

Rice noodles contain no fat and are an ideal substitute for egg noodles.

Beef, Water Chestnut & Rice Soup

Serves 4 • CALORIES PER SERVING: 205 • FAT CONTENT PER SERVING: 4.5 G

INGREDIENTS

350 g/12 oz lean beef (such as rump or sirloin)
1 litre/$1^3/4$ pints/1 quart fresh beef stock
1 cinnamon stick, broken
2 star anise
2 tbsp dark soy sauce
2 tbsp dry sherry
3 tbsp tomato purée (paste)
115 g/4 oz can water chestnuts, drained and sliced
175 g/6 oz/3 cups cooked white rice
1 tsp zested orange rind
6 tbsp orange juice
salt and pepper

TO GARNISH:
strips of orange rind
2 tbsp chives, snipped

1 Carefully trim away any fat from the beef. Cut the beef into thin strips and then place into a large saucepan.

2 Pour over the stock and add the cinnamon, star anise, soy sauce, sherry, tomato purée (paste) and water chestnuts. Bring to the boil, skimming away any surface scum with a flat ladle. Cover the pan and simmer gently for about 20 minutes or until the beef is tender.

3 Skim the soup with a flat ladle to remove any scum again. Remove and discard the cinnamon and star anise. Blot the surface with absorbent kitchen paper to remove any fat.

4 Stir in the rice, orange rind and juice. Season with salt and pepper to taste. Heat through for 2–3 minutes before ladling into warm bowls. Serve the soup garnished with strips of orange rind and snipped chives.

VARIATION

Omit the rice for a lighter soup that is an ideal starter for an Oriental meal of many courses. For a more substantial soup that would be a meal in its own right, add diced vegetables such as carrot, (bell) pepper, sweetcorn or courgette (zucchini).

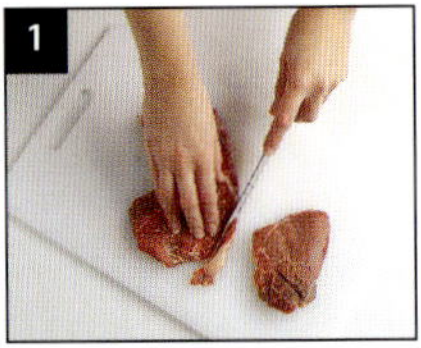

Winter Beef & Vegetable Soup

Serves 4 • CALORIES PER SERVING: 161 • FAT CONTENT PER SERVING: 3.3 G

INGREDIENTS

60 g/2 oz/1/3 cup pearl barley
1.2 litres/2 pints/5 cups fresh beef stock
1 tsp dried mixed herbs
225 g/8 oz lean rump or sirloin beef
1 large carrot, diced
1 leek, shredded
1 medium onion, chopped
2 sticks celery, sliced
salt and pepper
2 tbsp fresh parsley, chopped, to garnish
crusty bread, to serve

1 Place the pearl barley in a large saucepan. Pour over the stock and add the mixed herbs. Bring to the boil, cover and simmer for 10 minutes.

2 Trim any fat from the beef and cut the meat into thin strips.

3 Skim away any scum that has risen to the top of the stock.

4 Add the beef, carrot, leek, onion and celery to the pan. Bring back to the boil, cover and simmer for about 20 minutes or until the meat and vegetables are just tender.

5 Skim away any remaining scum that has risen to the top of the soup with a flat ladle. Blot the surface with absorbent kitchen paper to remove any fat. Season with salt and pepper to taste.

6 Ladle the soup into warm bowls and sprinkle with freshly chopped parsley. Serve accompanied with plenty of crusty bread.

VARIATION

This soup is just as delicious made with lean lamb or pork fillet. A vegetarian version can be made by omitting the beef and beef stock and using vegetable stock instead. Just before serving, stir in 175 g/ 6 oz fresh bean curd (tofu), drained and diced. An even more substantial soup can be made by adding other root vegetables, such as swede or turnip, instead of, or as well as, the carrot.

Mediterranean-style Fish Soup

Serves 4 • CALORIES PER SERVING: 270 • FAT CONTENT PER SERVING: 5.3 G

INGREDIENTS

1 tbsp olive oil
1 large onion, chopped
2 garlic cloves, finely chopped
425 ml/15 fl oz/$1^{3}/_{4}$ cups fresh fish stock
150 ml/5 fl oz/$^{2}/_{3}$ cup dry white wine
1 bay leaf
1 sprig each fresh thyme, rosemary and oregano
450 g/1 lb firm white fish fillets (such as cod, monkfish or halibut), skinned and cut into 2.5 cm/1 inch cubes
450 g/1 lb fresh mussels, prepared
400 g/14 oz can chopped tomatoes
225 g/8 oz peeled prawns (shrimp), thawed if frozen
salt and pepper
sprigs of thyme, to garnish

TO SERVE:
lemon wedges
4 slices toasted French bread, rubbed with cut garlic clove

1 Heat the oil in a large pan and gently fry the onion and garlic for 2–3 minutes until just softened.

2 Pour in the stock and wine and bring to the boil. Tie the bay leaf and herbs together with clean string and add to the saucepan together with the fish and mussels. Stir well, cover and simmer for 5 minutes.

3 Stir in the tomatoes and prawns (shrimp) and continue to cook for a further 3–4 minutes until piping hot and the fish is cooked through.

4 Discard the herbs and any mussels that have not opened. Season and ladle into warm bowls. Garnish with sprigs of thyme and serve with lemon wedges and toasted bread.

COOK'S TIP

Traditionally, the toasted bread is placed at the bottom of the bowl and the soup spooned over the top. For convenience, look out for prepared, cooked shellfish mixtures, which you could use instead of fresh fish. Simply add to the soup with the tomatoes in step 3.

Tuscan Bean & Vegetable Soup

Serves 4 • CALORIES PER SERVING: 156 • FAT CONTENT PER SERVING: 1.5 G

INGREDIENTS

1 medium onion, chopped
1 garlic clove, finely chopped
2 celery sticks, sliced
1 large carrot, diced
400 g/14 oz can chopped tomatoes
150 ml/5 fl oz/$^{2}/_{3}$ cup Italian dry red wine
1.2 litres/2 pints/5 cups fresh vegetable stock
1 tsp dried oregano
425 g/15 oz can mixed beans and pulses
2 medium courgettes (zucchini), diced
1 tbsp tomato purée (paste)
salt and pepper

TO SERVE:
low-fat pesto sauce (see page 146)
crusty bread

1 Place the onion, garlic, celery and carrot in a large saucepan. Stir in the tomatoes, red wine, vegetable stock and oregano.

2 Bring the vegetable mixture to the boil, cover and leave to simmer for 15 minutes. Stir the beans and courgettes (zucchini) into the mixture, and continue to cook, uncovered, for a further 5 minutes.

3 Add the tomato purée (paste) to the mixture and season well with salt and pepper to taste. Then heat through, stirring occasionally, for 2–3 minutes, but do not allow the mixture to boil again.

4 Ladle the soup into warm bowls and top with a spoonful of low-fat pesto on each portion. Serve the soup accompanied with plenty of fresh crusty bread.

VARIATION

For a more substantial soup, add 350 g/12 oz diced lean cooked chicken or turkey with the tomato purée (paste) in step 3.

Lentil, Pasta & Vegetable Soup

Serves 4 • CALORIES PER SERVING: 378 • FAT CONTENT PER SERVING: 4.9 G

INGREDIENTS

1 tbsp olive oil
1 medium onion, chopped
4 garlic cloves, finely chopped
350 g/12 oz carrot, sliced
1 stick celery, sliced
225 g/8 oz/1 1/4 cups red lentils
600 ml/1 pint/2 1/2 cups fresh vegetable stock
700 ml/1 1/4 pint/scant 3 cups boiling water
150 g/5 1/2 oz/scant 1 cup pasta
150 ml/5 fl oz/2/3 cup natural low-fat fromage frais (unsweetened yogurt)
salt and pepper
2 tbsp fresh parsley, chopped, to garnish

1 Heat the oil in a large saucepan and gently fry the prepared onion, garlic, carrot and celery, stirring gently, for 5 minutes until the vegetables begin to soften.

2 Add the lentils, stock and boiling water. Season with salt and pepper to taste, stir and bring back to the boil. Simmer, uncovered, for 15 minutes until the lentils are completely tender. Allow to cool for 10 minutes.

3 Meanwhile, bring another saucepan of water to the boil and cook the pasta according to the instructions on the packet. Drain well and set aside.

4 Place the soup in a blender and process until smooth. Return to a saucepan and add the pasta. Bring back to a simmer and heat for 2–3 minutes until piping hot. Remove from the heat and stir in the fromage frais (yogurt). Season if necessary.

5 Serve sprinkled with chopped parsley.

COOK'S TIP

Avoid boiling the soup once the fromage frais (yogurt) has been added. Otherwise it will separate and become watery, spoiling the appearance of the soup.

2

4

4

Creamy Sweetcorn Soup

Serves 4 • CALORIES PER SERVING: 346 • FAT CONTENT PER SERVING: 2.4 G

INGREDIENTS

1 large onion, chopped
1 large potato, peeled and diced
1 litre/$1\frac{3}{4}$ pints/1 quart skimmed milk
1 bay leaf
$\frac{1}{2}$ tsp ground nutmeg
450 g/1 lb sweetcorn kernels, canned or frozen, drained or thawed
1 tbsp cornflour (cornstarch)
3 tbsp cold water
4 tbsp natural low-fat fromage frais (unsweetened yogurt)
salt and pepper

TO GARNISH:
100 g/$3\frac{1}{2}$ oz lean ham, diced
2 tbsp fresh chives, snipped

1 Place the onion and potato in a large pan and pour over the milk. Add the bay leaf, nutmeg and half the sweetcorn. Bring to the boil, cover and simmer for 15 minutes until the potato is softened. Stir occasionally and keep the heat low so that the milk does not burn on the bottom of the pan.

2 Discard the bay leaf and leave the liquid to cool for 10 minutes. Transfer to a blender and process for a few seconds. Or, rub through a sieve.

3 Pour the smooth liquid into a pan. Blend the cornflour (cornstarch) with the water to make a paste and stir it into the soup.

4 Bring the soup back to the boil, stirring until it thickens, and add the remaining sweetcorn. Heat through for 2–3 minutes until piping hot.

5 Remove from the heat and season with salt and pepper to taste. Stir in the fromage frais (yogurt). Ladle the soup into warm bowls and serve sprinkled with the diced ham and snipped chives.

VARIATION

For a more substantial soup, add 225 g/8 oz flaked white crab meat or peeled prawns (shrimp) in step 4.

Tomato & Red (Bell) Pepper Soup

Serves 4 • CALORIES PER SERVING: 93 • FAT CONTENT PER SERVING: 1 G

INGREDIENTS

2 large red (bell) peppers
1 large onion, chopped
2 sticks celery, trimmed and chopped
1 garlic clove, crushed
600 ml/1 pint/2½ cups fresh vegetable stock
2 bay leaves
2 x 400 g/14 oz cans plum tomatoes
salt and pepper
2 spring onions (scallions), finely shredded, to garnish
crusty bread, to serve

1 Preheat the grill (broiler) to hot. Halve and deseed the (bell) peppers, arrange them on the grill (broiler) rack and cook, turning occasionally, for 8–10 minutes until softened and charred.

2 Leave to cool slightly, then carefully peel off the charred skin. Reserving a small piece for garnish, chop the (bell) pepper flesh and place in a large saucepan.

3 Mix in the onion, celery and garlic. Add the stock and the bay leaves. Bring to the boil, cover and simmer for 15 minutes. Remove from the heat.

4 Stir in the tomatoes and transfer to a blender. Process for a few seconds until smooth. Return to the saucepan.

5 Season to taste and heat for 3–4 minutes until piping hot. Ladle into warm bowls and garnish with the reserved (bell) pepper cut into strips and the spring onion (scallion). Serve with crusty bread.

COOK'S TIP

If you prefer a coarser, more robust soup, lightly mash the tomatoes with a wooden spoon and omit the blending process in step 4.

1

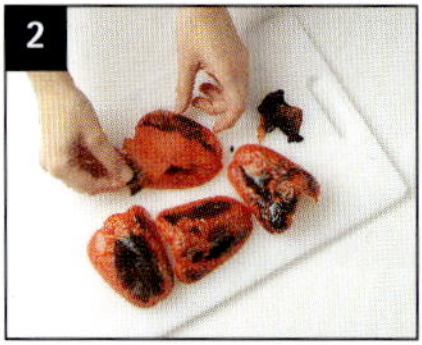
2

4

Carrot, Apple & Celery Soup

Serves 4 • CALORIES PER SERVING: 150 • FAT CONTENT PER SERVING: 1.4 G

INGREDIENTS

900 g/2 lb carrots, finely diced
1 medium onion, chopped
3 sticks celery, diced
1 litre/1 3/4 pints/1 quart fresh vegetable stock
3 medium-sized eating (dessert) apples
2 tbsp tomato purée (paste)
1 bay leaf
2 tsp caster (superfine) sugar
1/4 large lemon
salt and pepper
celery leaves, washed and shredded, to garnish

1 Place the carrots, onion and celery in a large saucepan and add the stock. Bring to the boil, cover and simmer for 10 minutes.

2 Meanwhile, peel, core and dice 2 of the eating (dessert) apples. Add the pieces of apple, tomato purée (paste), bay leaf and caster (superfine) sugar to the saucepan and bring to the boil. Reduce the heat, half cover and allow to simmer for 20 minutes. Remove and discard the bay leaf.

3 Meanwhile, wash, core and cut the remaining apple into thin slices, leaving on the skin. Place the apple slices in a small saucepan and squeeze over the lemon juice. Heat gently and simmer for 1–2 minutes until tender. Drain and set aside.

4 Place the carrot and apple mixture in a blender or food processor and blend until smooth. Alternatively, press the carrot and apple mixture through a sieve with the back of a wooden spoon.

5 Gently re-heat the soup if necessary and season with salt and pepper to taste. Ladle the soup into warm bowls and serve topped with the reserved apple slices and shredded celery leaves.

COOK'S TIP

Soaking light coloured fruit in lemon juice helps to prevent it from turning brown.

Chilled Piquant Prawn (Shrimp) & Cucumber Soup

Serves 4 • CALORIES PER SERVING: 104 • FAT CONTENT PER SERVING: 1 G

INGREDIENTS

1 cucumber, peeled and diced
400 ml/14 fl oz/$1^2/_3$ cups fresh fish stock, chilled
150 ml/5 fl oz/$^2/_3$ cup tomato juice
150 ml/5 fl oz/$^2/_3$ cup low-fat natural (unsweetened) yogurt
150 ml/5 fl oz/$^2/_3$ cup low-fat fromage frais (or double the quantity of yogurt)
125 g/$4^1/_2$ oz peeled prawns (shrimp), thawed if frozen, roughly chopped
few drops Tabasco sauce
1 tbsp fresh mint, chopped
salt and white pepper
ice cubes, to serve

TO GARNISH:
sprigs of mint
cucumber slices
whole peeled prawns (shrimp)

1 Place the diced cucumber in a blender or food processor and work for a few seconds until smooth. Alternatively, chop the cucumber finely and push through a sieve.

2 Transfer the cucumber to a bowl. Stir in the stock, tomato juice, yogurt, fromage frais (if using) and prawns (shrimp), and mix well. Add the Tabasco sauce and season with salt and pepper to taste.

3 Stir in the chopped mint, cover and chill for at least 2 hours.

4 Ladle the soup into glass bowls and add a few ice cubes. Serve garnished with sprigs of fresh mint, cucumber slices and whole peeled prawns (shrimp).

VARIATION

Instead of prawns (shrimp), add white crab meat or minced chicken. For a vegetarian version of this soup, omit the prawns (shrimp) and add an extra 125 g/4½ oz finely diced cucumber. Use fresh vegetable stock instead of fish stock.

Rosy Melon & Strawberries

Serves 4 • CALORIES PER SERVING: 83 • FAT CONTENT PER SERVING: 0.2 G

INGREDIENTS

$^1/_4$ honeydew melon
$^1/_2$ Charentais or Cantaloupe melon
150 ml/5 fl oz/$^2/_3$ cup rosé wine
2–3 tsp rose water
175 g/6 oz small strawberries, washed and hulled
rose petals, to garnish

1 Scoop out the seeds from both melons with a spoon. Then carefully remove the skin, taking care not to remove too much flesh.

2 Cut the melon flesh into thin strips and place in a bowl. Pour over the wine and sufficient rose water to taste. Mix together gently, cover and leave to chill in the refrigerator for at least 2 hours.

3 Halve the strawberries and carefully mix into the melon. Allow the melon and strawberries to stand at room temperature for about 15 minutes for the flavours to develop – if the melon is too cold, there will be little flavour.

4 Arrange on individual serving plates and serve sprinkled with a few rose petals, if wished.

COOK'S TIP

Rose water is a distillation of rose petals. It is generally available from large pharmacies and leading supermarkets as well as from more specialist food suppliers.

VARIATION

It does not matter whether the rosé wine is sweet or dry – although sweet wine contains more calories. Experiment with different types of melon. Varieties such as 'Sweet Dream' have whitish-green flesh, while Charentais melons, which have orange flesh, are fragrant and go better with a dry wine. If you wish, soak the strawberries in the wine with the melon, but always allow the fruit to return to room temperature before serving.

Italian Platter

Serves 4 • CALORIES PER SERVING: 175 • FAT CONTENT PER SERVING: 7.6 G

INGREDIENTS

125 g/4½ oz reduced-fat Mozzarella cheese, drained
60 g/2 oz lean Parma ham (prosciutto)
400 g/14 oz can artichoke hearts, drained
4 ripe figs
1 small mango
few plain Grissini (bread sticks), to serve

DRESSING:
1 small orange
1 tbsp passata (sieved tomatoes)
1 tsp wholegrain mustard
4 tbsp low-fat natural (unsweetened) yogurt
fresh basil leaves
salt and pepper

1 Cut the cheese into 12 sticks, 6.5 cm/2½ inches long. Remove the fat from the Parma ham (prosciutto) and slice the meat into 12 strips.

2 Carefully wrap a strip of Parma ham (prosciutto) around each stick of cheese and arrange them neatly on a large serving platter.

3 Halve the artichoke hearts and cut the figs into quarters. Arrange them on the serving platter in groups.

4 Peel the mango, then slice it down each side of the large, flat central stone. Slice the flesh into strips and arrange them so that they form a fan shape on the serving platter.

5 To make the dressing, pare the rind from half of the orange using a vegetable peeler. Cut the rind into small strips and place them in a bowl. Extract the juice from the orange and add it to the bowl containing the rind.

6 Add the passata (sieved tomatoes), mustard, yogurt and seasoning to the bowl and mix together. Shred the basil leaves and mix them into the dressing.

7 Spoon the dressing into a small dish and serve with the Italian Platter, accompanied with Grissini (bread sticks).

Breakfast Muffins

Serves 4 • CALORIES PER SERVING: 270 • FAT CONTENT PER SERVING: 12.3 G

INGREDIENTS

2 wholemeal muffins
8 rashers lean back bacon, rinds removed
4 medium eggs
2 large tomatoes
2 large flat mushrooms
4 tbsp fresh vegetable stock
salt and pepper
1 small bunch fresh chives, snipped, to garnish

1 Preheat the grill (broiler) to medium. Cut the muffins in half and lightly toast them for 1–2 minutes on the open side. Set aside and keep warm.

2 Trim off all visible fat from the bacon and grill for 2–3 minutes on each side until cooked through. Drain on absorbent kitchen paper and keep warm.

3 Place 4 egg-poaching rings in a frying pan (skillet) and pour in enough water to cover the base of the pan. Bring to the boil and reduce the heat to a simmer. Break one egg into each ring and poach for 5–6 minutes until set.

4 Cut the tomatoes into 8 thick slices and arrange on a piece of kitchen foil on the grill (broiler) rack. Grill (broil) for 2–3 minutes until just cooked. Season to taste.

5 Peel and thickly slice the mushrooms. Place in a saucepan with the stock, bring to the boil, cover and simmer for 4–5 minutes until cooked. Drain and keep warm.

6 To serve, arrange the tomato and mushroom slices on the toasted muffins and top each with 2 rashers of bacon. Arrange an egg on top of each and sprinkle with a little pepper. Garnish and serve at once.

VARIATION

Omit the bacon for a vegetarian version and use more tomatoes and mushrooms instead. Alternatively, include a grilled (broiled) low-fat tofu (bean curd) or Quorn burger.

3

4

5

Cheesy Ham & Celery Savoury

Serves 4 • CALORIES PER SERVING: 155 • FAT CONTENT PER SERVING: 6.9 G

INGREDIENTS

4 sticks celery
12 thin slices of lean ham
1 bunch spring onions (scallions)
175 g/6 oz low-fat soft cheese with garlic and herbs
6 tbsp low-fat natural (unsweetened) yogurt
4 tbsp Parmesan cheese, freshly grated
celery salt and pepper

TO SERVE:
tomato salad
crusty bread

1 Wash the celery, remove the leaves and slice the celery sticks into 3 equal portions.

2 Cut any visible fat off the ham and lay the slices on a chopping board. Place a piece of celery on each piece of ham and roll up. Place 3 ham and celery rolls in each of 4 small, heatproof dishes.

3 Trim the spring onions (scallions), then finely shred both the white and green parts. Sprinkle the spring onions (scallions) over the ham and celery rolls and season with celery salt and pepper.

4 Mix together the soft cheese and yogurt and spoon over the ham and celery rolls.

5 Preheat the grill (broiler) to medium. Sprinkle each portion with 1 tablespoon of grated Parmesan cheese and grill (broil) for 6–7 minutes until hot and the cheese has formed a crust. If the cheese starts to brown too quickly, lower the grill (broiler) setting slightly.

6 Serve with a tomato salad and crusty bread.

COOK'S TIP

Parmesan is useful in low-fat recipes because its intense flavour means you need to use only a small amount.

Parsleyed Chicken & Ham Pâté

Serves 4 • CALORIES PER SERVING: 132 • FAT CONTENT PER SERVING: 1.8 G

INGREDIENTS

225 g/8 oz lean, skinless chicken, cooked
100 g/$3\frac{1}{2}$ oz lean ham, trimmed
small bunch fresh parsley
1 tsp lime rind, grated
2 tbsp lime juice
1 garlic clove, peeled
125 ml/$4\frac{1}{2}$ fl oz/$\frac{1}{2}$ cup low-fat natural fromage frais (unsweetened yogurt)
salt and pepper
1 tsp lime zest, to garnish

TO SERVE:
wedges of lime
crisp bread

1 Dice the chicken and ham and place in a blender or food processor. Add the parsley, lime rind and juice, and garlic and process well until finely minced. Alternatively, finely chop the chicken, ham, parsley and garlic and place in a bowl. Mix gently with the lime rind and juice.

2 Transfer the mixture to a bowl and mix in the fromage frais (yogurt). Season with salt and pepper to taste, cover and leave to chill in the refrigerator for about 30 minutes.

3 Transfer the pâté to individual serving dishes and garnish with lime zest.

4 Serve the parsleyed chicken and ham pâtés with lime wedges and crisp bread.

VARIATION

This pâté can be made equally successfully with other kinds of minced, lean, cooked meat such as turkey, beef and pork. Alternatively, replace the chicken and ham with peeled prawns (shrimp) and/or white crab meat or with canned tuna in brine, drained. Remember that removing the skin from poultry reduces the fat content of any dish.

Spinach Cheese Moulds (Molds)

Serves 4 • CALORIES PER SERVING: 64 • FAT CONTENT PER SERVING: 0.2 G

INGREDIENTS

100 g/3½ oz fresh spinach leaves
300 g/10½ oz skimmed milk soft cheese
2 garlic cloves, crushed
sprigs of fresh parsley, tarragon and chives, finely chopped
salt and pepper

TO SERVE:
salad leaves and fresh herbs
pitta bread

1 Trim the stalks from the spinach leaves. Rinse the leaves under running water. Pack the leaves into a saucepan while still wet, cover and cook for 3–4 minutes until wilted – they will cook in the steam from the wet leaves (do not overcook). Drain well and pat dry with absorbent kitchen paper.

2 Base-line 4 small pudding basins or individual ramekin dishes with baking parchment. Line the basins or ramekins with spinach leaves so that the leaves overhang the edges if they are large enough to do so.

3 Place the cheese in a bowl and add the garlic and herbs. Mix together thoroughly and season to taste.

4 Spoon the cheese and herb mixture into the basins or ramekins and pull over the overlapping spinach to cover the cheese, or lay extra leaves to cover the top. Place a greaseproof (waxed) paper circle on top of each dish and weigh down with a 100 g/3½ oz weight. Leave to chill in the refrigerator for 1 hour.

5 Remove the weights and peel off the paper. Loosen the moulds (molds) gently by running a small palette knife (spatula) around the edges of each dish and turn them out on to individual serving plates. Serve with a mixture of salad leaves and fresh herbs, and warm pitta bread.

Soufflé Omelette

Serves 4 • CALORIES PER SERVING: 141 • FAT CONTENT PER SERVING: 9.7 G

INGREDIENTS

175 g/6 oz cherry tomatoes
225 g/8 oz mixed mushrooms (such as button, chestnut, shiitake, oyster and wild mushrooms)
4 tbsp fresh vegetable stock
small bunch fresh thyme
4 medium eggs, separated
4 medium egg whites
4 tsp olive oil
25 g/1 oz rocket (arugula) leaves
salt and pepper
fresh thyme sprigs, to garnish

1 Halve the tomatoes and place them in a pan. Wipe the mushrooms with kitchen paper, trim if necessary and slice if large. Place in the pan.

2 Add the stock and thyme to the pan, and season to taste with salt and pepper. Bring to the boil, cover and simmer for 5–6 minutes until tender. Drain, remove the thyme and discard, and keep the mixture warm.

3 Meanwhile, whisk the egg yolks with 8 tablespoons of water until frothy. In a clean, grease-free bowl, mix the 8 egg whites until stiff and dry.

4 Spoon the egg yolk mixture into the egg whites and, using a metal spoon, fold the whites and yolks into each other until well mixed. Take care not to knock out too much of the air.

5 For each omelette, brush a small omelette pan with 1 teaspoon of oil and heat until hot. Pour in a quarter of the egg mixture and cook for 4–5 minutes or until the mixture has set.

6 Preheat the grill (broiler) to medium and finish cooking the omelette for 2–3 minutes.

7 Transfer the omelette to a warm serving plate. Fill the omelette with a few rocket (arugula) leaves, and a quarter of the mushroom and tomato mixture. Flip over the top of the omelette, garnish with sprigs of thyme and serve.

Grilled Rice & Tuna (Bell) Peppers

Serves 4 • CALORIES PER SERVING: 383 • FAT CONTENT PER SERVING: 6.8 G

INGREDIENTS

60 g/2 oz/$^1/_3$ cup wild rice
60 g/2 oz/$^1/_3$ cup brown rice
4 assorted medium (bell) peppers
200 g/7 oz can tuna fish in brine, drained and flaked
325 g/11$^1/_2$ oz can sweetcorn kernels (with no added sugar or salt), drained
100 g/3$^1/_2$ oz reduced-fat Cheddar cheese, grated
1 bunch fresh basil leaves, shredded
2 tbsp dry white breadcrumbs
1 tbsp Parmesan cheese, freshly grated
salt and pepper
fresh basil leaves, to garnish
crisp salad leaves, to serve

1 Place the 2 rices in different saucepans, cover with water and cook according to the instructions on the packet. Drain well.

2 Meanwhile, preheat the grill (broiler) to medium. Halve the (bell) peppers, remove the seeds and stalks and arrange the peppers on the grill (broiler) rack, cut side down. Cook for 5 minutes, turn over and cook for a further 4–5 minutes.

3 Transfer the cooked rice to a mixing bowl and add the flaked tuna and drained sweetcorn. Gently fold in the grated Cheddar. Mix in the basil leaves and season to taste.

4 Divide the tuna and rice mixture into 8 equal portions. Pile each portion into each cooked (bell) pepper half. Mix together the breadcrumbs and Parmesan cheese and sprinkle the mixture over each (bell) pepper.

5 Place the (bell) peppers back under the grill (broiler) for 4–5 minutes until hot and golden-brown. Serve immediately, garnished with fresh basil leaves and accompanied with fresh, crisp salad leaves.

2

3

4

Baked Potatoes with a Spicy Filling

Serves 4 • CALORIES PER SERVING: 354 • FAT CONTENT PER SERVING: 5.9 G

INGREDIENTS

4 baking potatoes, each about 300 g/10½ oz
1 tbsp vegetable oil (optional)
400 g/14 oz can chick-peas (garbanzo beans), drained
1 tsp ground coriander
1 tsp ground cumin
4 tbsp fresh coriander (cilantro), chopped
150 ml/5 fl oz/⅔ cup low-fat natural (unsweetened) yogurt
salt and pepper
salad, to serve

1 Preheat the oven to 200°C/400°F/Gas Mark 6. Scrub the potatoes and pat them dry with absorbent kitchen paper. Prick them all over with a fork, brush with oil (if using) and season.

2 Place the potatoes on a baking sheet (cookie sheet) and bake for 1–1¼ hours or until cooked through. Leave to cool for 10 minutes.

3 Meanwhile, mash the chick-peas (garbanzo beans) with a fork or potato masher. Stir in the spices and half the chopped coriander (cilantro). Cover and set aside.

4 Halve the cooked potatoes and scoop the flesh into a bowl, keeping the shells intact. Mash the flesh until smooth and gently mix into the chick-pea (garbanzo bean) mixture with the yogurt. Season well.

5 Fill the potato shells with the potato and chick-pea (garbanzo bean) mixture. Return the potatoes to the oven and bake for 10–15 minutes until heated through. Serve sprinkled with the remaining chopped coriander (cilantro) and a fresh salad.

COOK'S TIP

For an even lower fat version of this recipe, bake the potatoes without oiling them first.

Spinach Crêpes with Curried Crab

Serves 4 • CALORIES PER SERVING: 259 • FAT CONTENT PER SERVING: 5.9 G

INGREDIENTS

115 g/4 oz buckwheat flour
1 large egg, beaten
300 ml/$^{1}/_{2}$ pint/1$^{1}/_{4}$ cups skimmed milk
125 g/4$^{1}/_{2}$ oz frozen spinach, thawed, well-drained and chopped
2 tsp vegetable oil

FILLING:
350 g/12 oz white crab meat
1 tsp mild curry powder
1 tbsp mango chutney
1 tbsp reduced-calorie mayonnaise
2 tbsp low-fat natural (unsweetened) yogurt
2 tbsp fresh coriander (cilantro), chopped

TO SERVE:
green salad
lemon wedges

1 Sift the flour into a bowl and remove any husks that remain in the sieve (strainer).

2 Make a well in the centre of the flour and add the egg. Gradually whisk in the milk, then blend in the spinach. Transfer the batter to a jug and let stand for 30 minutes.

3 To make the filling, mix together all the ingredients, except the coriander (cilantro), in a bowl, cover and chill.

4 Whisk the batter. Brush a small crêpe pan with a little oil, heat until hot and pour in enough batter to cover the base thinly. Cook for 1–2 minutes until set, turn over and cook for 1 minute until golden. Transfer to a warmed plate. Repeat to make 8 pancakes, layering them on the plate with baking parchment.

5 Stir the coriander (cilantro) into the crab mixture. Fold each pancake into quarters. Open one fold and fill with the crab mixture. Serve warm, with a green salad and lemon wedges.

VARIATION

Try lean diced chicken in a light white sauce or peeled prawns (shrimp) instead of the crab.

2

3

5

Meat & Poultry

The increased interest in healthy eating means that most supermarkets and butchers now offer special cuts of lean meat. Although they are often slightly more expensive than standard cuts, it is worth buying this meat and spending a little extra time cooking it carefully to enhance the flavour. You will not need to buy as much if you combine the meat with thoughtfully chosen and prepared vegetables.

Look out, too, for packs of low- or reduced-fat minced (ground) meat in your local supermarket, and include it in burgers or serve it in a flavour-filled sauce with rice or your favourite pasta.

Cut any visible fat from beef and pork before you cook it. Chicken and turkey are lower in fat than red meats, and you can make them even healthier by removing the skin. Duck is a rich meat with a distinctive flavour, and you need only a small amount to create apparently extravagant, flavourful dishes that are healthy, too.

Pan-cooked Pork with Fennel & Aniseed

Serves 4 • CALORIES PER SERVING: 242 • FAT CONTENT PER SERVING: 6.4 G

INGREDIENTS

- 4 lean pork chops, 125 g/ 4$^{1}/_{2}$ oz each
- 60 g/2 oz/$^{1}/_{3}$ cup brown rice, cooked
- 1 tsp orange rind, grated
- 4 spring onions (scallions), trimmed and finely chopped
- $^{1}/_{2}$ tsp aniseed
- 1 tbsp olive oil
- 1 fennel bulb, trimmed and thinly sliced
- 450 ml/16 fl oz/2 cups unsweetened orange juice
- 1 tbsp cornflour (cornstarch)
- 2 tbsp Pernod
- salt and pepper
- fennel fronds, to garnish
- cooked vegetables, to serve

1 Trim away any excess fat from the pork chops. Using a small, sharp knife, make a slit in the centre of each chop to create a pocket.

2 Mix the rice, orange rind, spring onions (scallions), salt and pepper to taste and aniseed together in a bowl. Press the mixture into the pocket of each chop, then press gently to seal.

3 Heat the oil in a frying pan (skillet) and fry the pork chops on each side for 2–3 minutes until lightly browned.

4 Add the sliced fennel and orange juice to the pan, bring to the boil and simmer for 15–20 minutes until the meat is tender and cooked through. Remove the pork and fennel with a slotted spoon and transfer to a serving plate.

5 Blend the cornflour (cornstarch) and Pernod together in a small bowl. Add the cornflour (cornstarch) mixture to the pan and stir into the pan juices. Cook for 2–3 minutes, stirring, until the sauce thickens.

6 Pour the Pernod sauce over the pork chops, garnish with fennel fronds and serve with a selection of cooked vegetables.

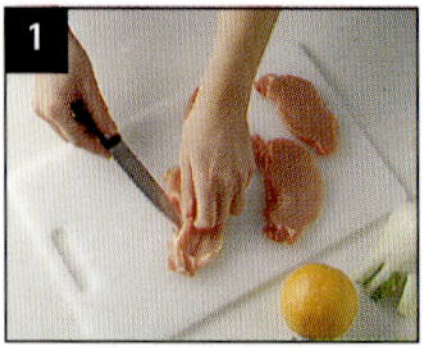

Pork Stroganoff

Serves 4 • Calories per serving: 197 • Fat content per serving: 7 g

INGREDIENTS

350 g/12 oz lean pork fillet
1 tbsp vegetable oil
1 medium onion, chopped
2 garlic cloves, crushed
25 g/1 oz plain (all-purpose) flour
2 tbsp tomato purée (paste)
425 ml/15 fl oz/1¾ cups fresh chicken or vegetable stock
125 g/4½ oz button mushrooms, sliced
1 large green (bell) pepper, deseeded and diced
½ tsp ground nutmeg
4 tbsp low-fat natural (unsweetened) yogurt, plus extra to serve
salt and pepper
white rice, freshly boiled, to serve
ground nutmeg and chopped parsley, to garnish

1 Trim away any excess fat and silver skin from the pork, then cut the meat into slices about 1 cm/½ inch thick.

2 Heat the oil in a large frying pan (skillet) and gently fry the pork, onion and garlic for 4–5 minutes until lightly browned.

3 Stir in the flour and tomato purée (paste), pour in the stock and stir to mix thoroughly.

4 Add the mushrooms, (bell) pepper, seasoning and nutmeg. Bring to the boil, cover and simmer for 20 minutes or until the pork is tender and cooked through.

5 Remove the saucepan from the heat and stir in the yogurt.

6 Garnish the boiled rice with chopped parsley. Spoon extra yogurt on top of the pork and mushrooms and dust with a little ground nutmeg.

COOK'S TIP

You can buy ready-made meat, vegetable and fish stocks from leading supermarkets. Although more expensive they are better nutritionally than stock cubes which are high in salt and artificial flavourings. However, home-made stock is best of all.

Pan-cooked Pork Medallions with Apples & Cider

Serves 4 • CALORIES PER SERVING: 192 • FAT CONTENT PER SERVING: 5.7 G

INGREDIENTS

8 lean pork medallions, about 50 g/1³/4 oz each
2 tsp vegetable oil
1 medium onion, finely sliced
1 tsp caster (superfine) sugar
1 tsp dried sage
150 ml/5 fl oz/²/3 cup dry (hard) cider
150 ml/5 fl oz/²/3 cup fresh chicken or vegetable stock
1 green-skinned apple
1 red-skinned apple
1 tbsp lemon juice
salt and pepper
fresh sage leaves, to garnish
freshly cooked vegetables, to serve

1 Discard the string from the pork and trim away any excess fat. Re-tie with clean string and set aside until required.

2 Heat the oil in a frying pan (skillet) and gently fry the onion for 5 minutes until softened. Add the sugar and cook for 3–4 minutes until golden.

3 Add the pork to the pan and cook for 2 minutes on each side until browned. Add the sage, cider and stock. Bring to the boil and then simmer for 20 minutes.

4 Meanwhile, core and cut each apple into 8 wedges. Toss the apple wedges in lemon juice so that they do not turn brown.

5 Add the apples to the pork and mix gently. Season and cook for 3–4 minutes until tender.

6 Remove the string from the pork and serve immediately, garnished with fresh sage and accompanied with freshly cooked vegetables.

COOK'S TIP

If pork medallions are not available, buy 400g/14 oz pork fillet and slice it into evenly-sized medallions yourself.

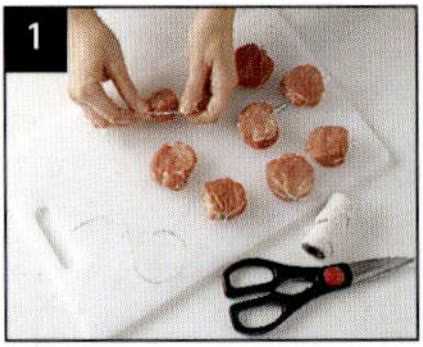

Red Roast Pork with (Bell) Peppers

Serves 4 • Calories per serving: 282 • Fat content per serving: 5 g

INGREDIENTS

450 g/1 lb lean pork fillets
6 tbsp dark soy sauce
2 tbsp dry sherry
1 tsp five-spice powder
2 garlic cloves, crushed
2.5 cm/1 inch piece root (fresh) ginger, finely chopped
1 large red (bell) pepper
1 large yellow (bell) pepper
1 large orange (bell) pepper
4 tbsp caster (superfine) sugar
2 tbsp red wine vinegar

TO GARNISH:
spring onions (scallions), shredded
fresh chives, snipped

1 Trim away excess fat and silver skin from the pork and place in a shallow dish.

2 Mix together the soy sauce, sherry, five-spice powder, garlic and ginger. Spoon over the pork, cover and marinate in the refrigerator for at least 1 hour.

3 Preheat the oven to 190°C/375°F/Gas Mark 5. Drain the pork, reserving the marinade. Place the pork on a roasting rack over a roasting tin (pan). Cook in the oven, occasionally basting with the marinade, for 1 hour or until cooked through.

4 Meanwhile, halve and deseed the (bell) peppers. Cut each (bell) pepper half into 3 equal portions. Arrange them on a baking sheet (cookie sheet) and bake alongside the pork for the last 30 minutes of the cooking time.

5 Place the caster (superfine) sugar and vinegar in a small saucepan and heat gently until the sugar dissolves. Bring to the boil and simmer for 3–4 minutes, until syrupy.

6 As soon as the pork is cooked, remove it from the oven and brush liberally with the sugar syrup. Leave to stand for 5 minutes, then slice and arrange on a warm serving platter with the (bell) peppers. Garnish and serve.

Pork with Ratatouille Sauce

Serves 4 • CALORIES PER SERVING: 214 • FAT CONTENT PER SERVING: 5.6 G

INGREDIENTS

4 lean, boneless pork chops, about 125 g/4½ oz each
1 tsp dried mixed herbs
salt and pepper
baked potatoes, to serve

SAUCE:
1 medium onion
1 garlic clove
1 small green (bell) pepper
1 small yellow (bell) pepper
1 medium courgette (zucchini)
100 g/3½ oz button mushrooms
400 g/14 oz can chopped tomatoes
2 tbsp tomato purée (paste)
1 tsp dried mixed herbs
1 tsp caster (superfine) sugar

1 To make the sauce, peel and chop the onion and garlic. Deseed and dice the (bell) peppers. Trim and dice the courgette (zucchini). Wipe and halve the mushrooms.

2 Place all of the vegetables in a saucepan and stir in the chopped tomatoes and tomato purée (paste). Add the dried herbs, sugar and plenty of seasoning. Bring to the boil, cover and simmer for 20 minutes.

3 Meanwhile, preheat the grill (broiler) to medium. Trim away any excess fat from the chops, then season on both sides and rub in the dried mixed herbs. Cook the chops for 5 minutes, then turn over and cook for a further 6–7 minutes or until cooked through.

4 Drain the chops on absorbent kitchen paper and serve accompanied with the sauce and baked potatoes.

COOK'S TIP

This vegetable sauce could be served with any other grilled (broiled) or baked meat or fish. It would also make an excellent alternative filling for the Spinach Crêpes on page 46.

Beef & Orange Curry

Serves 4 • CALORIES PER SERVING: 283 • FAT CONTENT PER SERVING: 10.5 G

INGREDIENTS

1 tbsp vegetable oil
225 g/8 oz shallots, halved
2 garlic cloves, crushed
450 g/1 lb lean rump or sirloin beef, trimmed and cut into 2 cm/3/4 inch cubes
3 tbsp curry paste
450 ml/16 fl oz/2 cups fresh beef stock
4 medium oranges
2 tsp cornflour (cornstarch)
salt and pepper
2 tbsp fresh coriander (cilantro), chopped, to garnish
basmati rice, freshly boiled, to serve

RAITA:
1/2 cucumber, finely diced
3 tbsp fresh mint, chopped
150 ml/5 fl oz/2/3 cup low-fat natural (unsweetened) yogurt

1 Heat the oil in a large saucepan. Gently fry the shallots, garlic and the cubes of beef for 5 minutes, stirring occasionally, until the beef is evenly browned all over.

2 Blend together the curry paste and stock. Add the mixture to the beef and stir to mix. Bring to the boil, cover and simmer for 1 hour or until the meat is tender.

3 Meanwhile, grate the rind of one orange. Extract the juice from the orange and from a second orange. Peel the two remaining oranges, removing as much pith as possible. Slice between each segment and remove the flesh.

4 Blend the cornflour (cornstarch) with the orange juice. At the end of the cooking time, stir the orange rind into the beef along with the orange and cornflour (cornstarch) mixture. Bring to the boil and simmer, stirring, for 3–4 minutes until the sauce thickens. Season and stir in the orange segments.

5 To make the raita, mix the cucumber with the mint and stir in the yogurt. Season. Garnish the curry and serve with rice and the raita.

Pan-seared Beef with Ginger, Pineapple & Chilli

Serves 4 • CALORIES PER SERVING: 191 • FAT CONTENT PER SERVING: 5.1 G

INGREDIENTS

4 lean beef steaks (such as rump, sirloin or fillet), 100 g/3$^1/_2$ oz each
2 tbsp ginger wine
2.5 cm/1 inch piece root (fresh) ginger, finely chopped
1 garlic clove, crushed
1 tsp ground chilli
1 tsp vegetable oil
salt and pepper
red chilli strips, to garnish

TO SERVE:
freshly cooked noodles
2 spring onions (scallions), shredded

RELISH:
225 g/8 oz fresh pineapple
1 small red (bell) pepper
1 red chilli
2 tbsp light soy sauce
1 piece stem ginger in syrup, drained and chopped

1 Trim any excess fat from the beef. Using a meat mallet or covered rolling pin, pound the steaks until 1 cm/½ inch thick. Season on both sides and place in a shallow dish.

2 Mix the ginger wine, root (fresh) ginger, garlic and chilli and pour over the meat. Cover and chill for 30 minutes.

3 To make the relish, peel and finely chop the pineapple and place it in a bowl. Halve, deseed and finely chop the (bell) pepper and chilli. Stir into the pineapple together with the soy sauce and stem ginger. Cover and chill.

4 Brush a grill (broiler) pan with the oil and heat until hot. Drain the beef and add to the pan, pressing down to seal. Lower the heat and cook for 5 minutes. Turn the steaks over and cook for 5 minutes.

5 Drain the steaks on kitchen paper and transfer to serving plates. Garnish with chilli strips, and serve with noodles, spring onions (scallions) and the relish.

Beef & Tomato Gratin

Serves 4 • CALORIES PER SERVING: 319 • FAT CONTENT PER SERVING: 10.3 G

INGREDIENTS

350 g/12 oz lean beef, minced (ground)
1 large onion, finely chopped
1 tsp dried mixed herbs
1 tbsp plain (all-purpose) flour
300 ml/$^1/_2$ pint/1 $^1/_4$ cups beef stock
1 tbsp tomato purée (paste)
2 large tomatoes, thinly sliced
4 medium courgettes (zucchini), thinly sliced
2 tbsp cornflour (cornstarch)
300 ml/$^1/_2$ pint/1 $^1/_4$ cups skimmed milk
150 ml/5 fl oz/$^2/_3$ cup low-fat natural fromage frais (unsweetened yogurt)
1 medium egg yolk
4 tbsp Parmesan cheese, freshly grated
salt and pepper

1 Preheat the oven to 190°C/375°F/Gas Mark 5. In a large pan, dry-fry the beef and onion for 4–5 minutes until browned.

2 Stir in the herbs, flour, stock and tomato purée (paste), and season. Bring to the boil and simmer for 30 minutes until thickened.

3 Transfer the beef mixture to an ovenproof gratin dish. Cover with a layer of the sliced tomatoes and then add a layer of sliced courgettes (zucchini). Set aside until required.

4 Blend the cornflour (cornstarch) with a little milk in a small bowl. Pour the remaining milk into a saucepan and bring to the boil. Add the cornflour (cornstarch) mixture and cook, stirring, for 1–2 minutes until thickened. Remove from the heat and beat in the fromage frais (yogurt) and egg yolk. Season well.

5 Place the dish on to a baking sheet (cookie sheet) and spread the white sauce over the layer of courgettes (zucchini). Sprinkle with grated Parmesan and bake in the oven for 25–30 minutes until golden-brown. Serve immediately.

Sweet & Sour Venison Stir-fry

Serves 4 • CALORIES PER SERVING: 174 • FAT CONTENT PER SERVING: 1.9 G

INGREDIENTS

1 bunch spring onions (scallion)
1 red (bell) pepper
100 g/3 1/2 oz mangetout (snow peas)
100 g/3 1/2 oz baby sweetcorn cobs
350 g/12 oz lean venison steak
1 tbsp vegetable oil
1 clove garlic, crushed
2.5 cm/1 inch piece root (fresh) ginger, finely chopped
3 tbsp light soy sauce, plus extra for serving
1 tbsp white wine vinegar
2 tbsp dry sherry
2 tsp clear honey
225 g/8 oz can pineapple pieces in natural juice, drained
25 g/1 oz beansprouts
freshly cooked rice, to serve

1 Trim the spring onions (scallions) and cut into 2.5 cm/1 inch pieces. Halve and deseed the (bell) pepper and cut it into 2.5 cm/1 inch pieces. Top and tail the mangetout (snow peas) and trim the baby corn.

2 Trim the excess fat from the meat and cut it into thin strips. Heat the oil in a large frying pan (skillet) or wok until hot and stir-fry the meat, garlic and ginger for 5 minutes.

3 Add the spring onion (scallion), (bell) pepper, mangetout (snow peas) and baby corn to the pan, then add the soy sauce, vinegar, sherry and honey. Stir-fry for 5 minutes, keeping the heat high.

4 Carefully stir in the pineapple pieces and beansprouts and cook for a further 1–2 minutes to heat through. Serve with freshly cooked rice and extra soy sauce for dipping.

VARIATION

For a quick and nutritious meal-in-one, cook 225 g/8 oz egg noodles in boiling water for 3–4 minutes. Drain well and add to the pan in step 4, together with the pineapple and beansprouts. Stir well to mix. You will have to add an extra 2 tbsp soy sauce with the pineapple and beansprouts so that the stir-fry does not dry out.

2

2

4

Venison & Garlic Mash

Serves 4 • CALORIES PER SERVING: 503 • FAT CONTENT PER SERVING: 6.1 G

INGREDIENTS

8 medallions of venison, 75 g/2^3/4 oz each
1 tbsp vegetable oil
1 red onion, chopped
150 ml/5 fl oz/^{2}/3 cup fresh beef stock
150 ml/5 fl oz/^{2}/3 cup red wine
3 tbsp redcurrant jelly
100 g/3^1/2 oz no-need-to-soak dried, pitted prunes
2 tsp cornflour (cornstarch)
2 tbsp brandy
salt and pepper
patty pans, to serve (optional)

GARLIC MASH:
900 g/2 lb potatoes, peeled and diced
^{1}/2 tsp garlic purée (paste)
2 tbsp low-fat natural fromage frais (unsweetened yogurt)
4 tbsp fresh parsley, chopped

1 Trim off any excess fat from the meat and season with salt and pepper on both sides.

2 Heat the oil in a pan and fry the medallions with the onions on a high heat for 2 minutes on each side until brown.

3 Lower the heat and pour in the stock and wine. Add the redcurrant jelly and prunes and stir until the jelly melts. Bring to the boil, cover and simmer for 10 minutes until cooked through.

4 Meanwhile, make the garlic mash. Place the potatoes in a saucepan and cover with water. Bring to the boil and cook for 8–10 minutes until tender. Drain.

5 Mash the potatoes until smooth. Add the garlic purée (paste), fromage frais (yogurt) and parsley and blend thoroughly. Season, set aside and keep warm.

6 Remove the medallions from the pan with a slotted spoon and keep warm.

7 Blend the cornflour (cornstarch) with the brandy in a small bowl and add to the pan juices. Heat, stirring, until thickened. Season to taste. Serve the venison with the sauce and garlic mash.

Venison Meatballs with Sherried Kumquat Sauce

Serves 4 • CALORIES PER SERVING: 178 • FAT CONTENT PER SERVING: 2.1 G

INGREDIENTS

450 g/1 lb lean venison, minced (ground)
1 small leek, finely chopped
1 medium carrot, finely grated
1/2 tsp ground nutmeg
1 medium egg white, lightly beaten
salt and pepper

TO SERVE:
freshly cooked pasta or noodles
freshly cooked vegetables

SAUCE:
100 g/3 1/2 oz kumquats
15 g/1/2 oz caster (superfine) sugar
150 ml/5 fl oz/2/3 cup water
4 tbsp dry sherry
1 tsp cornflour (cornstarch)

1 Place the venison in a mixing bowl together with the leek, carrot, seasoning and nutmeg. Add the egg white and bind the ingredients together with your hands until the mixture is well moulded and firm.

2 Divide the mixture into 16 equal portions. Using your fingers, form each portion into a small round ball.

3 Bring a large saucepan of water to the boil. Arrange the meatballs on a layer of baking parchment in a steamer or large sieve (strainer) and place over the boiling water. Cover and steam for 10 minutes until cooked through.

4 Meanwhile, make the sauce. Wash and thinly slice the kumquats. Place them in a saucepan with the sugar and water and bring to the boil. Simmer for 2–3 minutes until just tender.

5 Blend the sherry and cornflour (cornstarch) together and add to the pan. Heat through, stirring, until the sauce thickens. Season to taste.

6 Drain the meatballs and transfer to a serving plate. Spoon over the sauce and serve.

Fruity Lamb Casserole

Serves 4 • Calories per serving: 280 • Fat content per serving: 11.6 g

INGREDIENTS

450 g/1 lb lean lamb, trimmed and cut into 2.5 cm/1 inch cubes
1 tsp ground cinnamon
1 tsp ground coriander
1 tsp ground cumin
2 tsp olive oil
1 medium red onion, finely chopped
1 garlic clove, crushed
400 g/14 oz can chopped tomatoes
2 tbsp tomato purée (paste)
125 g/4½ oz no-soak dried apricots
1 tsp caster (superfine) sugar
300 ml/½ pint/1¼ cups vegetable stock
salt and pepper
1 small bunch fresh coriander (cilantro), to garnish
brown rice, steamed couscous or bulgar wheat, to serve

1 Preheat the oven to 180°C/350°F/Gas Mark 4. Place the meat in a mixing bowl and add the spices and oil. Mix thoroughly so that the lamb is well coated in the spices.

2 Heat a non-stick frying pan (skillet) for a few seconds until it is hot, then add the spiced lamb. Reduce the heat and cook for 4–5 minutes, stirring, until browned all over. Using a slotted spoon, remove the lamb and transfer to a large ovenproof casserole.

3 In the same frying pan (skillet), cook the onion, garlic, tomatoes and tomato purée (paste) for 5 minutes. Season to taste. Stir in the apricots and sugar, add the stock and bring to the boil.

4 Spoon the sauce over the lamb and mix well. Cover and cook in the oven for 1 hour, removing the lid for the last 10 minutes.

5 Roughly chop the coriander (cilantro) and sprinkle over the casserole to garnish. Serve with brown rice, steamed couscous or bulgar wheat.

Lamb, (Bell) Pepper, & Couscous

Serves 4 • CALORIES PER SERVING: 522 • FAT CONTENT PER SERVING: 12.5 G

INGREDIENTS

2 medium red onions, sliced
juice of 1 lemon
1 large red (bell) pepper, deseeded and thickly sliced
1 large green (bell) pepper, deseeded and thickly sliced
1 large orange (bell) pepper, deseeded and thickly sliced
pinch of saffron strands
cinnamon stick, broken
1 tbsp clear honey
300 ml/$^{1}/_{2}$ pint/1$^{1}/_{4}$ cups vegetable stock
2 tsp olive oil
350 g/12 oz lean lamb fillet, trimmed and sliced
1 tsp Harissa paste
200 g/7 oz can chopped tomatoes
425 g/15 oz can chick-peas (garbanzo beans), drained
350 g/12 oz precooked couscous
2 tsp ground cinnamon
salt and pepper

1 Toss the onions in the lemon juice and transfer to a saucepan. Mix in the (bell) peppers, saffron, cinnamon stick and honey. Pour in the stock, bring to the boil, cover and simmer for 5 minutes.

2 Meanwhile, heat the oil in a frying pan (skillet) and gently fry the lamb for 3–4 minutes until browned all over.

3 Using a slotted spoon, drain the lamb and transfer it to the pan with the onions and peppers. Season and stir in the Harissa paste, tomatoes and chick-peas (garbanzo beans). Mix well, bring back to the boil and simmer, uncovered, for 20 minutes.

4 Meanwhile, soak the couscous, following the instructions on the packet. Bring a saucepan of water to the boil. Transfer the couscous to a steamer or sieve (strainer) lined with muslin (cheesecloth) and place over the pan of boiling water. Cover and steam as directed.

5 Transfer the couscous to a warm serving platter and dust with ground cinnamon. Remove and discard the cinnamon stick. Spoon the stew over the couscous to serve.

Hot Pot Chops

Serves 4 • CALORIES PER SERVING: 252 • FAT CONTENT PER SERVING: 11.3 G

INGREDIENTS

4 lean, boneless lamb leg steaks, about 125 g/4$^1/_2$ oz each
1 small onion, thinly sliced
1 medium carrot, thinly sliced
1 medium potato, thinly sliced
1 tsp olive oil
1 tsp dried rosemary
salt and pepper
fresh rosemary, to garnish
freshly steamed green vegetables, to serve

1 Preheat the oven to 180°C/350°F/Gas Mark 4. Using a sharp knife, trim any excess fat from the lamb steaks.

2 Season both sides of the steaks with salt and pepper to taste and arrange them on a baking sheet (cookie sheet).

3 Alternate layers of sliced onion, carrot and potato on top of each lamb steak.

4 Brush the tops of the potato lightly with oil, season well with salt and pepper to taste and then sprinkle with a little dried rosemary.

5 Bake the hot pot chops in the oven for 25–30 minutes until the lamb is tender and cooked through.

6 Drain the lamb on absorbent kitchen paper and transfer to a warmed serving plate. Garnish with fresh rosemary and serve accompanied with a selection of green vegetables.

VARIATION

This recipe would work equally well with boneless chicken breasts. Pound the chicken slightly with a meat mallet or covered rolling pin so that the pieces are the same thickness throughout.

1

3

4

Minty Lamb Burgers

Serves 4 • CALORIES PER SERVING: 237 • FAT CONTENT PER SERVING: 7.8 G

INGREDIENTS

350 g/12 oz lean lamb, minced (ground)
1 medium onion, finely chopped
4 tbsp dry wholemeal breadcrumbs
2 tbsp mint jelly
salt and pepper

TO SERVE:
4 wholemeal baps, split
2 large tomatoes, sliced
small piece of cucumber, sliced
lettuce leaves

RELISH:
4 tbsp low-fat natural fromage frais (unsweetened yogurt)
1 tbsp mint jelly, softened
5 cm/2 inch piece of cucumber, finely diced
1 tbsp fresh mint, chopped

1 Place the lamb in a large bowl and mix in the onion, breadcrumbs and jelly. Season well, then mould the ingredients together with your hands to form a firm mixture.

2 Divide the mixture into 4 and shape each portion into a round measuring 10 cm/4 inches across. Place the rounds on a plate lined with baking parchment and leave to chill for 30 minutes.

3 Preheat the grill (broiler) to medium. Line a grill (broiler) rack with baking parchment, securing the ends under the rack, and place the burgers on top. Cook for 8 minutes, then turn over the burgers and cook for a further 7 minutes or until cooked through.

4 Meanwhile, make the relish. Mix together the fromage frais (unsweetened yogurt), mint jelly, cucumber and freshly chopped mint in a bowl. Cover and leave to chill in the refrigerator until required.

5 Drain the burgers on absorbent kitchen paper. Serve the burgers inside the baps with sliced tomatoes, cucumber, lettuce and relish.

Tricolour Chicken & Spinach Lasagne

Serves 4 • CALORIES PER SERVING: 424 • FAT CONTENT PER SERVING: 7.2 G

INGREDIENTS

350 g/12 oz frozen chopped spinach, thawed and drained
$^1/_2$ tsp ground nutmeg
450 g/1 lb lean, cooked chicken meat, skinned and diced
4 sheets no-pre-cook lasagne verde
$1^1/_2$ tbsp cornflour (cornstarch)
425 ml/15 fl oz/$1^3/_4$ cups skimmed milk
4 tbsp Parmesan cheese, freshly grated
salt and pepper

TOMATO SAUCE:
400 g/14 oz can chopped tomatoes
1 medium onion, chopped
1 garlic clove, crushed (minced)
150 ml/5 fl oz/$^2/_3$ cup white wine
3 tbsp tomato purée (paste)
1 tsp dried oregano

1 Preheat the oven to 200°C/400°F/Gas Mark 6. To make the tomato sauce, place the tomatoes in a pan and stir in the onion, garlic, wine, tomato purée (paste) and oregano. Bring to the boil and simmer for 20 minutes until thick. Season.

2 Drain the spinach again and spread it out on kitchen paper to absorb any excess water. Layer the spinach in the base of an ovenproof dish. Sprinkle with nutmeg and season.

3 Arrange the chicken over the spinach and spoon over the tomato sauce. Arrange the lasagne over the tomato sauce.

4 Blend the cornflour (cornstarch) with a little of the milk to make a paste. Pour the remaining milk into a pan and stir in the cornflour (cornstarch) paste. Heat for 2–3 minutes, stirring, until the sauce thickens. Season well.

5 Spoon the sauce over the lasagne and transfer the dish to a baking sheet (cookie sheet). Sprinkle the grated cheese over the sauce and bake for 25 minutes until golden.

Chicken Pasta Bake with Fennel & Raisins

Serves 4 • CALORIES PER SERVING: 521 • FAT CONTENT PER SERVING: 15.5 G

INGREDIENTS

- 2 bulbs fennel
- 2 medium red onions, shredded
- 1 tbsp lemon juice
- 125 g/4½ oz button mushrooms
- 1 tbsp olive oil
- 225 g/8 oz penne (quills)
- 60 g/2 oz/⅓ cup raisins
- 225 g/8 oz lean, boneless cooked chicken, skinned and shredded
- 375 g/13 oz low-fat soft cheese with garlic and herbs
- 125 g/4½ oz low-fat Mozzarella cheese, thinly sliced
- 2 tbsp Parmesan cheese, grated
- salt and pepper

1 Preheat the oven to 200°C/400°F/Gas Mark 6. Trim the fennel, reserving the green fronds for garnishing, and slice the bulbs thinly. Coat the onions in the lemon juice. Quarter the mushrooms.

2 Heat the oil in a large frying pan (skillet) and fry the fennel, onion and mushrooms for 4–5 minutes, stirring, until just softened. Season and transfer the vegetable mixture to a large bowl.

3 Bring a pan of lightly salted water to the boil and cook the penne (quills) according to the instructions on the packet until 'al dente' (just cooked). Drain and mix the pasta with the vegetables.

4 Stir the raisins and chicken into the pasta mixture. Soften the soft cheese by beating it, then mix into the pasta and chicken – the heat from the pasta should make the cheese melt slightly.

5 Put the mixture into an ovenproof dish and transfer to a baking sheet (cookie sheet). Arrange the Mozzarella on top and sprinkle with the Parmesan. Bake for 20–25 minutes until golden. Garnish with fennel fronds and serve.

1

4

5

Baked Southern-style Chicken & Chips

Serves 4 • CALORIES PER SERVING: 402 • FAT CONTENT PER SERVING: 7.4 G

INGREDIENTS

4 baking potatoes, each 225 g/8 oz
1 tbsp sunflower oil
2 tsp coarse sea salt
2 tbsp plain (all-purpose) flour
pinch of cayenne pepper
1/2 tsp paprika pepper
1/2 tsp dried thyme
8 chicken drumsticks, skin removed
1 medium egg, beaten
2 tbsp cold water
6 tbsp dry white breadcrumbs
salt and pepper

TO SERVE:
low-fat coleslaw salad
sweetcorn relish

1 Preheat the oven to 200°C/400°F/Gas Mark 6. Wash and scrub the potatoes and cut each into 8 equal portions. Place in a clean plastic bag and add the oil. Seal and shake well to coat.

2 Arrange the potato wedges, skin side down, on a non-stick baking sheet (cookie sheet), sprinkle over the sea salt and bake in the oven for 30–35 minutes until they are tender and golden-brown.

3 Meanwhile, mix the flour, cayenne, paprika, thyme and salt and pepper to taste together on a plate. Press the chicken drumsticks into the seasoned flour to lightly coat all over.

4 On one plate mix together the egg and water. On another plate sprinkle the breadcrumbs. Dip the chicken drumsticks first in the egg and then in the breadcrumbs. Place on a non-stick baking sheet (cookie sheet).

5 Bake the chicken drumsticks alongside the potato wedges for 30 minutes, turning after 15 minutes, until they are tender and cooked through.

6 Drain the potato wedges thoroughly on absorbent kitchen paper to remove any excess fat. Serve the potato wedges with the chicken, accompanied by low-fat coleslaw and sweetcorn relish, if wished.

2

3

4

Lime Chicken Kebabs (Kabobs) with Mango Salsa

Serves 4 • CALORIES PER SERVING: 200 • FAT CONTENT PER SERVING: 1.5 G

INGREDIENTS

4 boneless chicken breasts, skinned, about 125 g/ $4^1/2$ oz each
3 tbsp lime marmalade
1 tsp white wine vinegar
$^1/2$ tsp lime rind, finely grated
1 tbsp lime juice
salt and pepper

TO SERVE:
lime wedges
boiled white rice, sprinkled with chilli powder

SALSA:
1 small mango
1 small red onion
1 tbsp lime juice
1 tbsp fresh coriander (cilantro), chopped

1 Slice the chicken breasts into thin pieces and thread on to 8 skewers so that the meat forms an S-shape down each skewer.

2 Preheat the grill (broiler) to medium. Arrange the chicken kebabs (kabobs) on the grill (broiler) rack. Mix together the marmalade, vinegar, lime rind and juice. Season with salt and pepper to taste. Brush the dressing over the chicken and grill (broil) for 5 minutes. Turn the chicken over, brush with the dressing again and grill (broil) for a further 4-5 minutes or until the chicken is cooked through.

3 Meanwhile, prepare the salsa. Peel the mango and slice the flesh off the smooth, central stone. Dice the flesh into small pieces and place in a small bowl.

4 Peel and finely chop the onion and mix into the mango, together with the lime juice and chopped coriander (cilantro). Season with salt and pepper to taste, cover and chill until required.

5 Serve the chicken kebabs (kabobs) with the salsa, accompanied with wedges of lime and boiled white rice sprinkled with chilli powder.

Sage Chicken & Rice

Serves 4 • CALORIES PER SERVING: 391 • FAT CONTENT PER SERVING: 3.9 G

INGREDIENTS

1 large onion, chopped
1 garlic clove, crushed
2 sticks celery, sliced
2 carrots, diced
2 sprigs fresh sage
300 ml/½ pint/1¼ cups chicken stock
350 g/12 oz boneless, skinless chicken breasts
225 g/8 oz/1⅓ cups mixed brown and wild rice
400 g/14 oz can chopped tomatoes
dash of Tabasco sauce
2 medium courgettes (zucchini), trimmed and thinly sliced
100 g/3½ oz lean ham, diced
salt and pepper
fresh sage, to garnish

TO SERVE:
salad leaves
crusty bread

1 Place the onion, garlic, celery, carrots and sprigs of fresh sage in a large saucepan and pour in the chicken stock. Bring to the boil, cover the pan and simmer for 5 minutes.

2 Cut the chicken into 2.5 cm/1 inch cubes and stir into the pan with the vegetables. Cover the pan and continue to cook for a further 5 minutes.

3 Stir in the rice and chopped tomatoes. Add a dash of Tabasco sauce to taste and season well. Bring to the boil, cover and simmer for 25 minutes.

4 Stir in the sliced courgettes (zucchini) and diced ham and continue to cook, uncovered, for a further 10 minutes, stirring occasionally, until the rice is just tender.

5 Remove and discard the sprigs of sage. Garnish with a few sage leaves and serve with a fresh salad and fresh crusty bread.

COOK'S TIP

If you do not have fresh sage, use 1 tsp of dried sage in step 1.

2

3

4

Chilli Chicken & Sweetcorn Meatballs

Serves 4 • CALORIES PER SERVING: 223 • FAT CONTENT PER SERVING: 3 G

INGREDIENTS

450 g/1 lb lean chicken, minced (ground)
4 spring onions (scallions), trimmed and finely chopped
1 small red chilli, deseeded and finely chopped
2.5 cm/1 inch piece root (fresh) ginger, finely chopped
100 g/3$^1/_2$ oz can sweetcorn (no added sugar or salt), drained
salt and white pepper
boiled jasmine rice, to serve

TO GARNISH:
spring onions (scallions) and red (bell) pepper, chopped

SAUCE:
150 ml/5 fl oz/$^2/_3$ cup fresh chicken stock
100 g/3$^1/_2$ oz cubed pineapple in natural juice, drained, with 4 tbsp reserved juice
1 medium carrot, cut into thin strips
1 small red (bell) pepper, deseeded and diced
1 small green (bell) pepper, deseeded and diced
1 tbsp light soy sauce
2 tbsp rice vinegar
1 tbsp caster (superfine) sugar
1 tbsp tomato purée (paste)
2 tsp cornflour (cornstarch) mixed to a paste with 4 tsp cold water

1 To make the meatballs, place the chicken in a bowl and add the spring onions (scallion), chilli, ginger, seasoning and sweetcorn. Mix together.

2 Divide the mixture into 16 portions and form each into a ball. Bring a pan of water to the boil. Arrange the meatballs on a sheet of baking parchment in a steamer or large sieve (strainer), place over the water, cover and steam for 10–12 minutes.

3 To make the sauce, pour the stock and pineapple juice into a pan and bring to the boil. Add the carrot, (bell) peppers and pineapple, cover and simmer for 5 minutes. Stir in the other ingredients and heat through, stirring, until thickened. Season.

4 Drain the meatballs and transfer to a serving plate. Garnish and serve with rice and the sauce.

Crispy-Topped Stuffed Chicken

Serves 4 • CALORIES PER SERVING: 211 • FAT CONTENT PER SERVING: 3.8 G

INGREDIENTS

- 4 boneless chicken breasts, about150 g/5 1/2 oz each, skinned
- 4 sprigs fresh tarragon
- 1/2 small orange (bell) pepper, deseeded and sliced
- 1 1/2 small green (bell) pepper, deseeded and sliced
- 15 g/1/2 oz wholemeal breadcrumbs
- 1 tbsp sesame seeds
- 4 tbsp lemon juice
- 1 small red (bell) pepper, halved and deseeded
- 200 g/7 oz can chopped tomatoes
- 1 small red chilli, deseeded and chopped
- 1/4 tsp celery salt
- salt and pepper
- fresh tarragon, to garnish

1 Preheat the oven to 200°C/400°F/Gas Mark 6. Slit the chicken breasts with a sharp knife to create a pocket in each. Season inside each pocket.

2 Place a sprig of tarragon and a few slices of orange and green (bell) peppers in each pocket. Place the chicken breasts on a baking sheet (cookie sheet) and sprinkle over the breadcrumbs and sesame seeds.

3 Spoon 1 tbsp lemon juice over each chicken breast and bake in the oven for 35–40 minutes until the chicken is cooked through.

4 Preheat the grill (broiler) to hot. Arrange the red (bell) pepper halves, skin side up, on the rack and cook for 5–6 minutes until the skin blisters. Cool for 10 minutes; peel off the skins.

5 Put the red (bell) pepper in a blender, add the tomatoes, chilli and celery salt and process for a few seconds. Season to taste. Alternatively, finely chop the red (bell) pepper and press through a sieve with the tomatoes and chilli.

6 When the chicken is cooked, heat the sauce, spoon a little on to a warm plate and arrange a chicken breast in the centre. Garnish with tarragon and serve.

Chicken with a Curried Yogurt Crust

Serves 4 • CALORIES PER SERVING: 176 • FAT CONTENT PER SERVING: 2 G

INGREDIENTS

1 garlic clove, crushed
2.5 cm/1 inch piece root (fresh) ginger, finely chopped
1 fresh green chilli, deseeded and finely chopped
6 tbsp low-fat natural (unsweetened) yogurt
1 tbsp tomato purée (paste)
1 tsp ground turmeric
1 tsp garam masala
1 tbsp lime juice
4 boneless, skinless chicken breasts, each 125 g/4 1/2 oz
salt and pepper
wedges of lime or lemon, to serve

RELISH:
4 medium tomatoes
1/4 cucumber
1 small red onion
2 tbsp fresh coriander (cilantro), chopped

1 Preheat the oven to 190°C/375°F/Gas Mark 5. In a small bowl mix together the garlic, ginger, chilli, yogurt, tomato purée (paste), turmeric, garam masala, lime juice and seasoning.

2 Wash and pat dry the chicken breasts and place them on a baking sheet (cookie sheet). Brush or spread the spicy yogurt mix over the chicken and bake in the oven for 30–35 minutes until the meat is tender and cooked through.

3 Meanwhile, make the relish. Finely chop the tomatoes, cucumber and onion and mix together with the coriander (cilantro). Season, cover and chill until required.

4 Drain the cooked chicken on absorbent kitchen paper and serve hot with the relish. Or, allow to cool, chill for at least 1 hour and serve sliced as part of a salad.

VARIATION

The spicy yogurt coating would work just as well if spread on a chunky white fish, such as cod fillet. The cooking time should be reduced to 15–20 minutes.

Grilled Chicken with Lemon & Honey

Serves 4 • CALORIES PER SERVING: 403 • FAT CONTENT PER SERVING: 4.7 G

INGREDIENTS

4 boneless chicken breasts, about 125 g/4$\frac{1}{2}$ oz each
2 tbsp clear honey
1 tbsp dark soy sauce
1 tsp lemon rind, finely grated
1 tbsp lemon juice
salt and pepper

TO GARNISH:
1 tbsp fresh chives, chopped
lemon rind, grated

NOODLES:
225 g/8 oz rice noodles
2 tsp sesame oil
1 tbsp sesame seeds
1 tsp lemon rind, finely grated

1 Preheat the grill (broiler) to medium. Skin and trim the chicken breasts to remove any excess fat, then wash and pat dry with absorbent kitchen paper. Using a sharp knife, score the chicken breasts with a criss-cross pattern on both sides (making sure that you do not cut all the way through the meat).

2 Mix together the honey, soy sauce, lemon rind and juice in a small bowl, and then season well with black pepper.

3 Arrange the chicken breasts on the grill (broiler) rack and brush with half of the honey mixture. Cook for 10 minutes, turn over and brush with the remaining mixture. Cook for a further 8–10 minutes or until cooked through.

4 Meanwhile, prepare the noodles according to the instructions on the packet. Drain well and transfer to a warm serving bowl. Mix the noodles with the sesame oil, sesame seeds and the lemon rind. Season and keep warm.

5 Drain the chicken and serve with a small mound of noodles, garnished with freshly chopped chives and grated lemon rind.

1

3

4

Chicken & Plum Casserole

Serves 4 • CALORIES PER SERVING: 285 • FAT CONTENT PER SERVING: 6.4 G

INGREDIENTS

- 2 rashers lean back bacon, rinds removed, trimmed and chopped
- 1 tbsp sunflower oil
- 450 g/1 lb skinless, boneless chicken thighs, cut into 4 equal strips
- 1 garlic clove, crushed
- 175 g/6 oz shallots, halved
- 225 g/8 oz plums, halved or quartered (if large) and stoned
- 1 tbsp light muscovado sugar
- 150 ml/5 fl oz/$^2/_3$ cup dry sherry
- 2 tbsp plum sauce
- 450 ml/16 fl oz/2 cups fresh chicken stock
- 2 tsp cornflour (cornstarch) mixed with 4 tsp cold water
- 2 tbsp flat-leaf parsley, chopped, to garnish
- crusty bread, to serve

1 In a large, non-stick frying pan (skillet), dry fry the bacon for 2–3 minutes until the juices run out. Remove the bacon from the pan with a slotted spoon, set aside and keep warm until required.

2 In the same frying pan (skillet), heat the oil and fry the chicken with the garlic and shallots for 4–5 minutes, stirring occasionally, until well browned all over.

3 Return the bacon to the frying pan (skillet) and stir in the plums, sugar, sherry, plum sauce and stock. Bring to the boil and simmer for 20 minutes until the plums have softened and the chicken is cooked through.

4 Add the cornflour (cornstarch) mixture to the frying pan (skillet) and cook, stirring, for a further 2–3 minutes until thickened.

5 Spoon the casserole on to warm serving plates and garnish with chopped parsley. Serve with chunks of bread to mop up the fruity gravy.

VARIATION

Chunks of lean turkey or pork would also go well with this combination of flavours. The cooking time will remain the same.

Orange Turkey with Rice & Green Vegetables

Serves 4 • CALORIES PER SERVING: 354 • FAT CONTENT PER SERVING: 5.5 G

INGREDIENTS

1 tbsp olive oil
1 medium onion, chopped
450 g/1 lb skinless lean turkey (such as fillet), cut into thin strips
300 ml/$\frac{1}{2}$ pint/$1\frac{1}{4}$ cups unsweetened orange juice
1 bay leaf
225 g/8 oz small broccoli florets
1 large courgette (zucchini), diced
1 large orange
350 g/12 oz/6 cups cooked brown rice
salt and pepper
25 g/1 oz pitted black olives in brine, drained and quartered, to garnish

1 Heat the oil in a large frying pan (skillet) and fry the onion and turkey, stirring, for 4–5 minutes until lightly browned.

2 Pour in the orange juice and add the bay leaf and seasoning. Bring to the boil and simmer for 10 minutes.

3 Meanwhile, bring a large saucepan of water to the boil and cook the broccoli florets, covered, for 2 minutes. Add the diced courgette (zucchini), bring back to the boil, cover and cook for a further 3 minutes (do not overcook). Drain and set aside until required.

4 Using a sharp knife, peel off the skin and white pith from the orange. Slice down the orange to make thin, round slices, then cut each slice in half.

5 Stir the broccoli, courgette (zucchini), rice and orange slices into the turkey mixture. Gently mix together and heat through for 3–4 minutes until piping hot.

6 Transfer the turkey rice to serving plates and garnish with black olives.

Curried Turkey with Apricots & Sultanas

Serves 4 • CALORIES PER SERVING: 418 • FAT CONTENT PER SERVING: 7.9 G

INGREDIENTS

1 tbsp vegetable oil
1 large onion, chopped
450 g/1 lb skinless turkey breast, cut into cubes
3 tbsp mild curry paste
300 ml/$^{1}/_{2}$ pint/1$^{1}/_{4}$ cups fresh chicken stock
175 g/6 oz frozen peas
400 g/14 oz can apricot halves in natural juice
50 g/1$^{3}/_{4}$ oz/$^{1}/_{3}$ cup sultanas (golden raisins)
350 g/12 oz/6 cups basmati rice, freshly cooked
1 tsp ground coriander
4 tbsp fresh coriander (cilantro), chopped
1 green chilli, deseeded and sliced
salt and pepper

1 Heat the oil in a large saucepan and fry the onion and turkey for 4–5 minutes until the onion has softened and the turkey is a light golden colour.

2 Stir in the curry paste. Pour in the stock, stirring, and bring to the boil. Cover and simmer for 15 minutes. Stir in the peas and bring back to the boil. Cover and simmer for about 5 minutes.

3 Drain the apricots, reserving the juice, and cut into thick slices. Add to the curry, stirring in a little of the juice if the mixture is becoming dry. Add the sultanas (golden raisins) and cook for 2 minutes.

4 Mix the rice with the ground coriander and fresh coriander (cilantro), stir in the chilli and season with salt and pepper to taste. Transfer the rice to warm plates and top with the turkey curry.

VARIATION

Peaches can be used instead of the apricots if you prefer. Cook in exactly the same way.

Turkey Loaf with Courgettes (Zucchini) & Tomato

Serves 6 • CALORIES PER SERVING: 179 • FAT CONTENT PER SERVING: 2.7 G

INGREDIENTS

1 medium onion, finely chopped
1 garlic clove, crushed
900 g/2 lb lean turkey, minced (ground)
1 tbsp fresh parsley, chopped
1 tbsp fresh chives, chopped
1 tbsp fresh tarragon, chopped
1 medium egg white, lightly beaten
1 medium, 1 large courgette (zucchini)
2 medium tomatoes
salt and pepper
tomato and herb sauce, to serve

1 Preheat the oven to 190°C/375°F/Gas Mark 5 and line a non-stick loaf tin (pan) with parchment. Place the onion, garlic and turkey in a bowl, add the herbs and season. Mix, then add the egg white to bind.

2 Press half of the mixture into the base of the tin (pan). Slice the medium courgette (zucchini) and the tomatoes and arrange over the meat. Top with the rest of the turkey; press down.

3 Cover with a layer of foil and place in a roasting tin (pan). Pour in enough boiling water to come half-way up the sides of the loaf tin (pan). Bake for 1–1¼ hours, removing the foil for the last 20 minutes of cooking time. Test the loaf is cooked by inserting a skewer into the centre – the juices should run clear. The loaf will also shrink away from the sides of the tin (pan) when it is cooked through.

4 Trim the large courgette (zucchini). Using a vegetable peeler or hand-held metal cheese slicer, cut the courgette (zucchini) into thin strips. Bring a saucepan of water to the boil and blanch the ribbons for 1–2 minutes until tender. Drain and keep warm. Transfer the turkey loaf to a warm platter. Drape over the courgette (zucchini) strips and serve with a tomato and herb sauce.

2

3

4

Duck with Kiwi Fruit & Raspberries

Serves 4 • CALORIES PER SERVING: 286 • FAT CONTENT PER SERVING: 8.4 G

INGREDIENTS

450 g/1 lb boneless duck breasts, skin removed
2 tbsp raspberry vinegar
2 tbsp brandy
1 tbsp clear honey
1 tsp sunflower oil
2 kiwi fruit, peeled and sliced thinly
salt and pepper

SAUCE:
225 g/8 oz raspberries, thawed if frozen
300 ml/½ pint/1¼ cups rosé wine
2 tsp cornflour (cornstarch) blended with 4 tsp cold water

1 Preheat the grill (broiler) to medium. Skin and trim the duck breasts to remove any excess fat. Score the flesh in diagonal lines and pound it with a meat mallet or a covered rolling pin until it is 1.5 cm/¾ inch thick.

2 Place the duck breasts in a shallow dish. Mix together the vinegar, brandy and honey in a small bowl and spoon over the duck. Cover and leave to chill for about 1 hour.

3 Drain the duck, reserving the marinade, and place on the grill (broiler) rack. Season and brush with oil. Cook for 10 minutes, turn over, season and brush with oil again. Cook for 8–10 minutes until the meat is cooked through.

4 For the sauce, reserve 60 g/2 oz raspberries and place the rest in a pan. Add the reserved marinade and the wine. Bring to the boil and simmer for 5 minutes until slightly reduced.

5 Strain the sauce through a sieve, pressing the raspberries with the back of a spoon. Return the liquid to the pan and add the cornflour (cornstarch) paste. Heat through, stirring, until thickened. Add the reserved raspberries and season.

6 Slice the duck breast and arrange fanned out on warm serving plates, alternating with slices of kiwi fruit. Spoon over the sauce and serve.

1

2

4

Roast Duck with Apples & Apricots

Serves 4 • CALORIES PER SERVING: 313 • FAT CONTENT PER SERVING: 6.5 G

INGREDIENTS

4 duckling portions, 350 g/12 oz each
4 tbsp dark soy sauce
2 tbsp light muscovado sugar
2 red-skinned apples
2 green-skinned apples
juice of 1 lemon
2 tbsp clear honey
few bay leaves
salt and pepper
assorted fresh vegetables, to serve

SAUCE:
400 g/14 oz can apricots, in natural juice
4 tbsp sweet sherry

1 Preheat the oven to 190°C/375°F/Gas Mark 5. Wash the duck and trim away any excess fat. Place on a wire rack over a roasting tin (pan) and prick all over with a fork.

2 Brush the duck with the soy sauce. Sprinkle over the sugar and season with pepper. Cook in the oven, basting occasionally, for 50–60 minutes until the meat is cooked – the juices should run clear when a skewer is inserted into the thickest part of the meat.

3 Core the apples and cut each into 6 wedges. Place in a bowl and mix with the lemon juice and honey. Transfer to a small roasting tin (pan), add a few bay leaves and season. Cook alongside the duck, basting occasionally, for 20–25 minutes until tender. Discard the bay leaves.

4 To make the sauce, place the apricots in a blender or food processor together with the juice from the can and the sherry. Process for a few seconds until smooth. Alternatively, mash the apricots with a fork until smooth and mix with the juice and sherry.

5 Just before serving, heat the apricot purée (paste) in a pan. Remove the skin from the duck (if wished) and pat the flesh with kitchen paper to absorb any fat.

6 Serve the duck with the apple wedges and the apricot sauce, and accompanied with vegetables.

Fish & Shellfish

Naturally low in fat yet rich in minerals and proteins, white fish and shellfish will be regular and important ingredients in any low-fat diet. There are so many flavours and textures available that the possible combinations are endless.

White fish, such as monkfish, haddock, cod and turbot, are widely available and easy to cook. Shellfish, too, are low in fat and rich in flavour, and they can be cooked in a variety of ways to produce mouthwatering, low-fat dishes. Some fish – salmon, tuna, trout and mackerel, for example – are oily and should be eaten in moderation. They are rich in the fat-soluble vitamins A and D, however, and it is also believed that the oil in these fish is beneficial in breaking down cholesterol in the bloodstream.

Use this versatile ingredient in recipes that will soon become standards in your repertoire, from comforting Prawn (Shrimp) and Tuna Pasta Bake and Fish Cakes with Piquant Tomato Sauce to sophisticated Five-spice Salmon with Ginger Stir Fry and Skewered Oriental Shellfish.

Prawn (Shrimp) & Tuna Pasta Bake

Serves 4 • CALORIES PER SERVING: 470 • FAT CONTENT PER SERVING: 8.5 G

INGREDIENTS

225 g/8 oz tricolour pasta shapes
1 tbsp vegetable oil
1 bunch spring onions (scallions), trimmed and chopped
175 g/6 oz button mushrooms, sliced
400 g/14 oz can tuna in brine, drained and flaked
175 g/6 oz peeled prawns (shrimp), thawed if frozen
2 tbsp cornflour (cornstarch)
425 ml/15 fl oz/1$^{3}/_{4}$ cups skimmed milk
4 medium tomatoes, sliced thinly
25 g/1 oz fresh breadcrumbs
25 g/1 oz reduced-fat Cheddar cheese, grated
salt and pepper

1 Preheat the oven to 190°C/375°F/Gas Mark 5. Bring a large pan of water to the boil and cook the pasta according to the instructions on the packet. Drain well.

2 Heat the oil in a frying pan (skillet) and fry all but a handful of the spring onions (scallions) and all of the mushrooms, stirring, for 4–5 minutes until softened.

3 Place the cooked pasta in a bowl and mix in the spring onions (scallions), mushrooms, tuna and prawns (shrimp). Set aside until required.

4 Blend the cornflour (cornstarch) with a little milk to make a paste. Pour the remaining milk into a saucepan and stir in the paste. Heat, stirring, until the sauce begins to thicken. Season well.

5 Pour the sauce over the pasta mixture and stir until well combined. Transfer to the base of an ovenproof gratin dish and place on a baking sheet (cookie sheet).

6 Arrange the tomato slices over the pasta and sprinkle with the breadcrumbs and cheese. Bake for 25–30 minutes. Sprinkle with the reserved spring onions (scallions).

2

3

6

Fish Cakes with Piquant Tomato Sauce

Serves 4 • CALORIES PER SERVING: 320 • FAT CONTENT PER SERVING: 7.5 G

INGREDIENTS

450 g/1 lb potatoes, diced
225 g/8 oz haddock fillet
225 g/8 oz trout fillet
1 bay leaf
425 ml/15 fl oz/1^3/4 cups fresh fish stock
2 tbsp low-fat natural fromage frais (unsweetened yogurt)
4 tbsp fresh snipped chives
75 g/2^3/4 oz dry white breadcrumbs
1 tbsp sunflower oil
salt and pepper
freshly snipped chives, to garnish
lemon wedges and salad leaves, to serve

PIQUANT TOMATO SAUCE:
200 ml/7 fl oz/^{3}/4 cup passata (sieved tomatoes)
4 tbsp dry white wine
4 tbsp low-fat natural (unsweetened) yogurt
chilli powder

1 Place the potatoes in a pan and cover with water. Bring to the boil and cook for 10 minutes until tender. Drain and mash.

2 Place the fish in a pan with the bay leaf and stock. Bring to the boil and simmer for 7–8 minutes. Remove the fish and flake the flesh away from the skin.

3 Mix the fish with the potato, fromage frais (yogurt), chives and seasoning. Cool, then cover and chill for 1 hour.

4 Sprinkle the breadcrumbs on to a plate. Divide the fish mixture into 8 and form each portion into a patty, about 7.5 cm/3 inches in diameter. Press each fish cake into the breadcrumbs.

5 Brush a frying pan (skillet) with oil and fry the fish cakes for 6 minutes. Turn the fish cakes over and cook for a further 5–6 minutes until golden. Drain on kitchen paper and keep warm.

6 To make the sauce, heat the passata (sieved tomatoes) and wine. Season, remove from the heat and stir in the yogurt. Return to the heat, sprinkle with chilli powder and serve with the fish cakes.

3

4

5

Provençal-style Mussels

Serves 4 • CALORIES PER SERVING: 185 • FAT CONTENT PER SERVING: 6.5 G

INGREDIENTS

1 tbsp olive oil
1 large onion, finely chopped
1 garlic clove, finely chopped
1 small red (bell) pepper, deseeded and finely chopped
sprig of rosemary
2 bay leaves
400 g/14 oz can chopped tomatoes
150 ml/5 fl oz/$^2/_3$ cup white wine
1 courgette (zucchini), diced finely
2 tbsp tomato purée (paste)
1 tsp caster (superfine) sugar
50 g/1$^3/_4$ oz pitted black olives in brine, drained and chopped
675 g/1$^1/_2$ lb cooked New Zealand mussels in their shells
1 tsp orange rind
salt and pepper
2 tbsp chopped, fresh parsley, to garnish
crusty bread, to serve

1 Heat the oil in a large saucepan and gently fry the onion, garlic and (bell) pepper for 3–4 minutes until just softened.

2 Add the sprig of rosemary and the bay leaves to the saucepan with the tomatoes and 100 ml/ 3½ fl oz/⅓ cup wine. Season to taste, then bring to the boil and simmer for 15 minutes.

3 Stir in the courgette (zucchini), tomato purée (paste), sugar and olives. Simmer for about 10 minutes.

4 Meanwhile, bring a pan of water to the boil. Arrange the mussels in a steamer or a large sieve (strainer) and place over the water. Sprinkle with the remaining wine and the orange rind. Cover and steam until the mussels open (discard any that remain closed).

5 Remove the mussels with a slotted spoon and arrange on a warm serving plate. Discard the herbs and spoon the sauce over the mussels. Garnish with chopped fresh parsley and serve with fresh, crusty bread.

Fish & Rice with Dark Rum

Serves 4 • CALORIES PER SERVING: 575 • FAT CONTENT PER SERVING: 4.5 G

INGREDIENTS

450 g/1 lb firm white fish fillets (such as cod or monkfish), skinned and cut into 2.5 cm/1 inch cubes
2 tsp ground cumin
2 tsp dried oregano
2 tbsp lime juice
150 ml/5 fl oz/$^{2}/_{3}$ cup dark rum
1 tbsp dark muscovado sugar
3 garlic cloves, chopped finely
1 large onion, chopped
1 medium red (bell) pepper, deseeded and sliced into rings
1 medium green (bell) pepper, deseeded and sliced into rings
1 medium yellow (bell) pepper, deseeded and sliced into rings
1.2 litres/2 pints/5 cups fish stock
350 g/12 oz/2 cups long-grain rice
salt and pepper
crusty bread, to serve

TO GARNISH:
fresh oregano leaves
lime wedges

1 Place the cubes of fish in a bowl and add the cumin, oregano, salt and pepper, lime juice, rum and sugar. Mix well, cover and leave to chill for 2 hours.

2 Place the garlic, onion and (bell) peppers in a large pan. Pour over the stock and stir in the rice. Bring to the boil, cover and cook for 15 minutes.

3 Gently add the fish and the marinade juices to the pan. Bring back to the boil and simmer, uncovered, stirring occasionally but taking care not to break up the fish, for 10 minutes until the fish is cooked and the rice is just tender.

4 Season with salt and pepper to taste and transfer to a warm serving plate. Garnish with fresh oregano and lime wedges and serve with crusty bread.

VARIATION

If you prefer, use unsweetened orange juice in the marinade instead of the rum.

Seafood Stir-fry

Serves 4 • CALORIES PER SERVING: 205 • FAT CONTENT PER SERVING: 6.5 G

INGREDIENTS

- 100 g/3 1/2 oz small, thin asparagus spears, trimmed
- 1 tbsp sunflower oil
- 2.5 cm/1 inch piece root (fresh) ginger, cut into thin strips
- 1 medium leek, shredded
- 2 medium carrots, julienned
- 100 g/3 1/2 oz baby sweetcorn cobs, quartered lengthwise
- 2 tbsp light soy sauce
- 1 tbsp oyster sauce
- 1 tsp clear honey
- 450 g/1 lb cooked, assorted shellfish, thawed if frozen
- freshly cooked egg noodles, to serve

TO GARNISH:

- 4 large cooked prawns
- small bunch fresh chives, freshly snipped

1 Bring a small pan of water to the boil and blanch the asparagus for 1–2 minutes. Drain, set aside and keep warm.

2 Heat the oil in a wok or large frying pan (skillet) and stir-fry the ginger, leek, carrot and sweetcorn for 3 minutes.

3 Add the soy sauce, oyster sauce and honey to the wok or frying pan (skillet). Stir in the shellfish and stir-fry for 2–3 minutes until the vegetables are just tender and the shellfish are heated through. Add the blanched asparagus and stir-fry for about 2 minutes.

4 To serve, pile the cooked noodles on to 4 warm serving plates and spoon over the seafood and vegetable stir fry. Serve garnished with a large prawn and freshly snipped chives.

COOK'S TIP

When you are preparing dense vegetables, such as carrots and other root vegetables, for stir frying, slice them into thin, evenly sized pieces so that they cook quickly and at the same rate. Delicate vegetables, such as (bell) peppers, leeks and spring onions (scallions), do not need to be cut as thinly.

Smoky Fish Pie

Serves 4 • CALORIES PER SERVING: 510 • FAT CONTENT PER SERVING: 6 G

INGREDIENTS

900 g/2 lb smoked haddock or cod fillets
600 ml/1 pint/2 1/2 cups skimmed milk
2 bay leaves
115 g/4 oz button mushrooms, quartered
115 g/4 oz frozen peas
115 g/4 oz frozen sweetcorn kernels
675 g/1 1/2 lb potatoes, diced
5 tbsp low-fat natural (unsweetened) yogurt
4 tbsp chopped fresh parsley
60 g/2 oz smoked salmon, sliced into thin strips
3 tbsp cornflour (cornstarch)
25 g/1 oz smoked cheese, grated
salt and pepper

1 Preheat the oven to 200°C/400°F/Gas Mark 6. Place the fish in a pan and add the milk and bay leaves. Bring to the boil, cover and then simmer for 5 minutes.

2 Add the mushrooms, peas and sweetcorn to the pan, bring back to a simmer, cover and cook for 5–7 minutes. Leave to cool.

3 Place the potatoes in a pan, cover with water, boil and cook for 8 minutes. Drain and mash with a fork or a potato masher. Stir in the yogurt, parsley and seasoning. Set aside.

4 Using a slotted spoon, remove the fish from the pan. Flake the cooked fish away from the skin and place in an ovenproof gratin dish. Reserve the cooking liquid.

5 Drain the vegetables, reserving the cooking liquid, and stir into the fish with the salmon strips.

6 Blend a little cooking liquid into the cornflour (cornstarch) to make a paste. Transfer the rest of the liquid to a pan and add the paste. Heat through, stirring, until thickened. Discard the bay leaves and season to taste.

7 Pour the sauce over the fish and vegetables. Spoon over the mashed potato so that the fish is covered, sprinkle with cheese and bake for 25–30 minutes. Serve.

Seafood Spaghetti

Serves 4 • CALORIES PER SERVING: 400 • FAT CONTENT PER SERVING: 7 G

INGREDIENTS

2 tsp olive oil
1 small red onion, chopped finely
1 tbsp lemon juice
1 garlic clove, crushed
2 sticks celery, chopped finely
150 ml/5 fl oz/2/3 cup fresh fish stock
150 ml/5 fl oz/2/3 cup dry white wine
small bunch fresh tarragon
450 g/1 lb fresh mussels, prepared
225 g/8 oz fresh prawns (shrimp), peeled and deveined
225 g/8 oz baby squid, cleaned, trimmed and sliced into rings
8 small cooked crab claws, cracked and peeled
225 g/8 oz spaghetti
salt and pepper
2 tbsp chopped fresh tarragon, to garnish

1 Heat the oil in a large pan and fry the onion with the lemon juice, garlic and celery for 3–4 minutes until just softened.

2 Pour in the stock and wine. Bring to the boil and add the tarragon and mussels. Cover and simmer for 5 minutes. Add the prawns (shrimp), squid and crab claws to the pan, mix and cook for 3–4 minutes until the mussels have opened, the prawns (shrimp) are pink and the squid is opaque. Discard any mussels that have not opened and the tarragon.

3 Meanwhile, cook the spaghetti in a saucepan of boiling water according to the instructions on the packet. Drain well.

4 Add the spaghetti to the shellfish mixture and toss together. Season.

5 Transfer to warm serving plates and spoon over the cooking juices. Serve garnished with freshly chopped tarragon.

COOK'S TIP

Crab claws contain lean crab meat. Ask your fishmonger to crack the claws for you, leaving the pincers intact, because the shell is very tough.

Chilli- & Crab-stuffed Red Snapper

Serves 4 • CALORIES PER SERVING: 120 • FAT CONTENT PER SERVING: 1 G

INGREDIENTS

4 red snappers, cleaned and scaled, 175 g/6 oz each
2 tbsp dry sherry
salt and pepper
stir-fried shredded vegetables, to serve

STUFFING:
1 small red chilli
1 garlic clove
1 spring onion (scallion)
$^1/_2$ tsp finely grated lime rind
1 tbsp lime juice
100 g/3$^1/_2$ oz white crab meat, flaked

TO GARNISH:
wedges of lime
red chilli strips

1 Rinse the fish and pat dry on absorbent kitchen paper. Season inside and out and place in a shallow dish. Spoon over the sherry and set aside.

2 Meanwhile, make the stuffing. Carefully halve, deseed and finely chop the chilli. Place in a small bowl.

3 Peel and finely chop the garlic. Trim and finely chop the spring onion (scallion). Add to the chilli together with the grated lime rind, lime juice and the flaked crab meat. Season with salt and pepper to taste and combine. Spoon some of the stuffing into the cavity of each fish.

4 Bring a large pan of water to the boil. Arrange the fish in a steamer lined with baking parchment or in a large sieve (strainer) and place over the boiling water. Cover and steam for 10 minutes. Turn the fish over and steam for 10 minutes or until the fish is cooked.

5 Drain the fish and transfer to serving plates. Garnish with wedges of lime and serve with stir-fried vegetables.

COOK'S TIP

Always wash your hands thoroughly after handling chillies as they can irritate your skin and eyes.

Citrus Fish Kebabs (Kabobs)

Serves 4 • CALORIES PER SERVING: 335 • FAT CONTENT PER SERVING: 14.5 G

INGREDIENTS

450 g/1 lb firm white fish fillets (such as cod or monkfish)
450 g/1 lb thick salmon fillet
2 large oranges
1 pink grapefruit
1 bunch fresh bay leaves
1 tsp finely grated lemon rind
3 tbsp lemon juice
2 tsp clear honey
2 garlic cloves, crushed
salt and pepper

TO SERVE:
crusty bread
mixed salad

1 Skin the white fish and the salmon, rinse and pat dry on absorbent kitchen paper. Cut each fillet into 16 pieces.

2 Using a sharp knife, remove the skin and pith from the oranges and grapefruit. Cut out the segments of flesh, removing all remaining traces of the pith and dividing membrane.

3 Thread the pieces of fish alternately with the orange and grapefruit segments and the bay leaves on to 8 skewers. Place the kebabs (kabobs) in a shallow dish.

4 Mix together the lemon rind and juice, the honey and garlic. Pour over the fish kebabs (kabobs) and season well. Cover and chill for 2 hours, turning occasionally.

5 Preheat the grill (broiler) to medium. Remove the skewers from the marinade and place on the rack. Cook for 7–8 minutes, turning once, until cooked through.

6 Drain, transfer to serving plates and serve with crusty bread and a fresh salad.

VARIATION

This dish makes an unusual starter. Try it with any firm fish – swordfish or shark, for example – or with tuna for a meatier texture.

1

2

3

Seafood Pizza

Serves 4 • CALORIES PER SERVING: 315 • FAT CONTENT PER SERVING: 7 G

INGREDIENTS

145 g/5 oz standard pizza base mix
4 tbsp chopped fresh dill or 2 tbsp dried dill
fresh dill, to garnish

SAUCE:
1 large red (bell) pepper
400 g/14 oz can chopped tomatoes with onion and herbs
3 tbsp tomato purée (paste)
salt and pepper

TOPPING:
350 g/12 oz assorted cooked seafood, thawed if frozen
1 tbsp capers in brine, drained
25 g/1 oz pitted black olives in brine, drained
25 g/1 oz low-fat Mozzarella cheese, grated
1 tbsp grated, fresh Parmesan cheese

1 Preheat the oven to 200°C/400°F/Gas Mark 6. Place the pizza base mix in a bowl and stir in the dill. Make the dough according to the instructions on the packet.

2 Press the dough into a round measuring 25.5 cm/10 inches across on a baking sheet (cookie sheet) lined with baking parchment. Set aside to prove (rise).

3 Preheat the grill (broiler) to hot. To make the sauce, halve and deseed the (bell) pepper and arrange on a grill (broiler) rack. Cook for 8–10 minutes until softened and charred. Leave to cool slightly, peel off the skin and chop the flesh.

4 Place the tomatoes and (bell) pepper in a saucepan. Bring to the boil and simmer for 10 minutes. Stir in the tomato purée (paste) and season to taste.

5 Spread the sauce over the pizza base and top with the seafood. Sprinkle over the capers and olives, top with the grated cheeses and bake for 25–30 minutes. Garnish with sprigs of dill and serve hot.

2

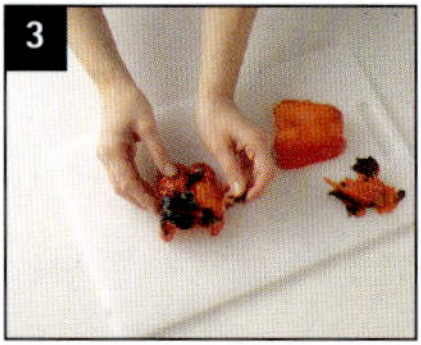
3

5

Pan-seared Halibut with Red Onion Relish

Serves 4 • CALORIES PER SERVING: 250 • FAT CONTENT PER SERVING: 8 G

INGREDIENTS

1 tsp olive oil
4 halibut steaks, skinned, 175 g/6 oz each
$^1/_2$ tsp cornflour (cornstarch) mixed with 2 tsp cold water
salt and pepper
2 tbsp fresh chives, snipped, to garnish

RED ONION RELISH:
2 medium red onions
6 shallots
1 tbsp lemon juice
2 tsp olive oil
2 tbsp red wine vinegar
2 tsp caster (superfine) sugar
150 ml/5 fl oz/$^2/_3$ cup fresh fish stock

1 To make the relish, peel and thinly shred the onions and shallots. Place in a small bowl and toss in the lemon juice.

2 Heat the oil in a pan and fry the onions and shallots for 3–4 minutes until just softened.

3 Add the vinegar and sugar and continue to cook for a further 2 minutes over a high heat. Pour in the stock and season well. Bring to the boil and simmer gently for a further 8–9 minutes until the sauce has thickened and is slightly reduced.

4 Brush a non-stick, ridged frying pan (skillet) with oil and heat until hot. Press the fish steaks into the pan to seal, lower the heat and cook for 4 minutes. Turn the fish over and cook for 4–5 minutes until cooked through. Drain on kitchen paper and keep warm.

5 Stir the cornflour (cornstarch) paste into the onion sauce and heat through, stirring, until thickened. Season to taste.

6 Pile the relish on to 4 warm serving plates and place a halibut steak on top of each. Garnish with chives and pepper.

Five-spice Salmon with Ginger Stir-fry

Serves 4 • Calories per serving: 295 • Fat content per serving: 18 g

INGREDIENTS

4 salmon fillets, skinned, 115 g/4 oz each
2 tsp five-spice powder
1 large leek
1 large carrot
115 g/4 oz mangetout (snow peas)
2.5 cm/1 inch piece root (fresh) ginger
2 tbsp ginger wine
2 tbsp light soy sauce
1 tbsp vegetable oil
salt and pepper
freshly boiled noodles, to serve

TO GARNISH:
shredded leek
shredded root (fresh) ginger
shredded carrot

1 Wash the salmon and pat dry on absorbent kitchen paper. Rub the five-spice powder into both sides of the fish and season with salt and pepper. Set aside until required.

2 Trim the leek, slice it down the centre and rinse under cold water to remove any dirt. Finely shred the leek. Peel the carrot and cut it into very thin strips. Top and tail the mangetout (snow peas) and cut them into shreds. Peel the ginger and slice thinly into strips.

3 Place all of the vegetables into a large bowl and toss in the ginger wine and 1 tablespoon of soy sauce. Set aside.

4 Preheat the grill (broiler) to medium. Place the salmon fillets on the rack and brush with the remaining soy sauce. Cook for 2–3 minutes on each side until cooked through.

5 While the salmon is cooking, heat the oil in a non-stick wok or large frying pan (skillet) and stir-fry the vegetables for 5 minutes until just tender. Take care that you do not overcook the vegetables – they should still have bite. Transfer to serving plates.

6 Drain the salmon on kitchen paper and serve on a bed of stir-fried vegetables. Garnish with shredded leek, ginger and carrot and serve.

Oriental Shellfish Kebabs (Kabobs)

Makes 12 • CALORIES PER SERVING: 100 • FAT CONTENT PER SERVING: 2.5 G

INGREDIENTS

350 g/12 oz raw tiger prawns (jumbo shrimp), peeled leaving tails intact
350 g/12 oz scallops, cleaned, trimmed and halved
1 bunch spring onions (scallions), sliced into 2.5 cm/1 inch pieces
1 red (bell) pepper, deseeded and cubed
100 g/3$^1/_2$ oz baby corn, trimmed and sliced into 1 cm/$^1/_2$ inch pieces
3 tbsp dark soy sauce
1$^1/_2$ tsp hot chilli powder
$^1/_2$ tsp ground ginger
1 tbsp sunflower oil
1 red chilli, deseeded and sliced

DIP:
4 tbsp dark soy sauce
4 tbsp dry sherry
2 tsp clear honey
2.5 cm/1 inch piece root (fresh) ginger, peeled and grated
1 spring onion (scallion), trimmed and very finely sliced

1 Soak 12 wooden skewers in cold water for 10 minutes to prevent them from burning.

2 Divide the prawns (shrimp), scallops, spring onions (scallions), (bell) pepper and baby corn cobs into 12 portions and thread on to the skewers. Cover the ends with foil so that they do not burn and place in a shallow dish.

3 Mix the soy sauce, chilli powder and ground ginger and coat the shellfish and vegetable kebabs (kabobs). Cover and leave to chill for about 2 hours.

4 Preheat the grill (broiler) to hot. Place the kebabs (kabobs) on the rack, brush the shellfish and vegetables with oil and cook for 2–3 minutes on each side until the prawns (shrimp) turn pink, the scallops become opaque and the vegetables are soft.

5 Mix together the dip ingredients.

6 Remove the foil and transfer the kebabs (kabobs) to a warm serving platter. Garnish with sliced chilli and serve with the dip.

2

3

3

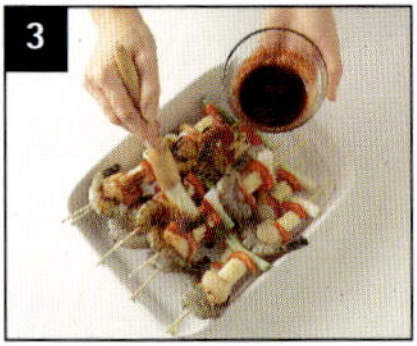

Tuna Steaks with Fragrant Spices & Lime

Serves 4 • CALORIES PER SERVING: 200 • FAT CONTENT PER SERVING: 3.5 G

INGREDIENTS

4 tuna steaks, 175 g/6 oz each
1/2 tsp finely grated lime rind
1 garlic clove, crushed
2 tsp olive oil
1 tsp ground cumin
1 tsp ground coriander
pepper
1 tbsp lime juice
fresh coriander (cilantro), to garnish

TO SERVE:
avocado relish (see Cook's Tip, below)
lime wedges
tomato wedges

1 Trim the skin from the tuna steaks, rinse and pat dry on absorbent kitchen paper.

2 In a small bowl, mix together the lime rind, garlic, olive oil, cumin, ground coriander and pepper to make a paste.

3 Spread the paste thinly on both sides of the tuna. Heat a non-stick, ridged frying pan (skillet) until hot and press the tuna steaks into the pan to seal them. Lower the heat and cook for 5 minutes. Turn the fish over and cook for a further 4–5 minutes until the fish is cooked through. Drain on absorbent kitchen paper and transfer to a serving plate.

4 Sprinkle the lime juice and chopped coriander (cilantro) over the fish.

5 Serve with freshly made avocado relish (see Cook's Tip, right), lime wedges and tomatoes.

COOK'S TIP

For low-fat avocado relish to serve with tuna, peel and remove the stone from one small ripe avocado. Toss in 1 tbsp lime juice. Mix in 1 tbsp freshly chopped coriander (cilantro) and 1 small finely chopped red onion. Stir in some chopped fresh mango or a chopped medium tomato and season well.

Baked Trout Mexican-style

Serves 4 • CALORIES PER SERVING: 235 • FAT CONTENT PER RECIPE: 5.5 G

INGREDIENTS

- 4 trout, 225 g/8 oz each
- 1 small bunch fresh coriander (cilantro)
- 4 shallots, shredded finely
- 1 small yellow (bell) pepper, deseeded and very finely chopped
- 1 small red (bell) pepper, deseeded and very finely chopped
- 2 green chillies, deseeded and finely chopped
- 1–2 red chillies, deseeded and finely chopped
- 1 tbsp lemon juice
- 1 tbsp white wine vinegar
- 2 tsp caster (superfine) sugar
- salt and pepper
- fresh coriander (cilantro), to garnish
- salad leaves, to serve

1 Preheat the oven to 180°C/350°F/Gas Mark 4. Wash the trout and pat dry with absorbent kitchen paper. Season the cavities with salt and pepper and fill with a few coriander (cilantro) leaves.

2 Place the fish side by side in a shallow ovenproof dish. Sprinkle over the shallots, (bell) peppers and chillies.

3 Mix together the lemon juice, vinegar and sugar in a bowl. Spoon over the trout and season to taste. Cover the dish and bake for 30 minutes or until the fish is tender and the flesh is opaque.

4 Remove the fish with a fish slice and drain. Transfer to warm serving plates and spoon the cooking juices over the fish. Garnish with fresh coriander (cilantro) and serve immediately with chilli bean rice, if you wish (see Cook's Tip, right).

COOK'S TIP

To make chilli bean rice to serve with this recipe, cook 225 g/8 oz/1¼ cup long-grain white rice in boiling water. Drain and return to the pan. Drain and rinse a 400 g/14 oz can kidney beans and stir into the rice along with 1 tsp each of ground cumin and ground coriander. Stir in 4 tbsp freshly chopped coriander (cilantro) and season well.

Vegetables & Salads

Too frequently, leaf vegetables are overcooked and limp, with all the goodness and flavour boiled out, while salads are often nothing more than a dismal leaf or two of pale green lettuce with a slice of tomato and a dry ring of onion. Make the most of the wonderful range of fresh produce that is available in our shops and markets.

Steam broccoli and cabbage so that they are colourful and crunchy. Enjoy the wonderfully appetizing shades of orange and yellow (bell) peppers and the almost unbelievable purple-brown of aubergine (eggplant). Trying grating root vegetables – carrots and daikon or mooli – to add flavour and texture to garnishes and casseroles. Look out for red and curly lettuces to bring excitement to an enticing summer salad. Use sweet baby tomatoes in salads and on skewers, and raid your garden and windowsill for sprigs of fresh mint and basil leaves.

Nuts and seeds are high in fat, so both should be used in moderation. However, they are a valuable source of protein and minerals, and vegetarians and vegans in particular need to ensure that their diets contain these valuable ingredients.

Vegetable Spaghetti with Lemon Dressing

Serves 4 • CALORIES PER SERVING: 330 • FAT CONTENT PER SERVING: 2.5 G

INGREDIENTS

225 g/8 oz celeriac
2 medium carrots
2 medium leeks
1 small red (bell) pepper
1 small yellow (bell) pepper
2 garlic cloves
1 tsp celery seeds
1 tbsp lemon juice
300 g/$10^1/2$ oz spaghetti
celery leaves, chopped, to garnish

LEMON DRESSING:
1 tsp finely grated lemon rind
1 tbsp lemon juice
4 tbsp low-fat natural fromage frais (unsweetened yogurt)
salt and pepper
2 tbsp snipped fresh chives

1 Peel the celeriac and carrots, cut into thin matchsticks and place in a bowl. Slice the leeks, rinse to flush out any trapped dirt, then shred finely. Halve, deseed and slice the (bell) peppers. Peel and thinly slice the garlic. Add these vegetables to the celeriac and the carrots.

2 Toss the vegetables with the celery seeds and lemon juice.

3 Bring a large pan of water to the boil and cook the spaghetti according to the instructions on the packet. Drain well and keep warm.

4 Bring another large saucepan of water to the boil, put the vegetables in a steamer or sieve (strainer) and place over the boiling water. Cover and steam for 6–7 minutes or until just tender.

5 When the spaghetti and vegetables are cooked, mix the ingredients for the lemon dressing together.

6 Transfer the spaghetti and vegetables to a warm serving bowl and mix with the dressing. Garnish with chopped celery leaves and serve.

1

2

4

Pesto Pasta

Serves 4 • CALORIES PER SERVING: 350 • FAT CONTENT PER SERVING: 4.5 G

INGREDIENTS

- 225 g/8 oz chestnut mushrooms, sliced
- 150 ml/5 fl oz/¾ cup fresh vegetable stock
- 175 g/6 oz asparagus, trimmed and cut into 5 cm/2 inch lengths
- 300 g/10½ oz green and white tagliatelle
- 400 g/14 oz canned artichoke hearts, drained and halved
- Grissini (bread sticks), to serve

TO GARNISH:
- basil leaves, shredded
- Parmesan shavings

PESTO:
- 2 large garlic cloves, crushed
- 15 g/½ oz fresh basil leaves, washed
- 6 tbsp low-fat natural fromage frais (unsweetened yogurt)
- 2 tbsp freshly grated Parmesan cheese
- salt and pepper

1 Place the mushrooms in a pan with the stock. Bring to the boil, cover and simmer for 3–4 minutes until tender. Drain; set aside.

2 Bring a small pan of water to the boil and cook the asparagus for 3–4 minutes until tender. Drain and set aside.

3 Bring a large pan of lightly salted water to the boil and cook the tagliatelle according to the instructions on the packet. Drain, return to the pan and keep warm.

4 Make the pesto. Place all of the ingredients in a blender or food processor and process for a few seconds until smooth. Alternatively, finely chop the basil and mix all the ingredients together.

5 Add the mushrooms, asparagus and artichoke hearts to the pasta and cook, stirring, over a low heat for 2–3 minutes. Remove from the heat, mix with the pesto and transfer to a warm bowl. Garnish with shredded basil leaves and Parmesan shavings and serve with Grissini (bread sticks), if wished.

Rice-stuffed Mushrooms

Serves 4 • CALORIES PER SERVING: 315 • FAT CONTENT PER SERVING: 6 G

INGREDIENTS

4 large flat mushrooms
100 g/3 1/2 oz assorted wild mushrooms, sliced
4 dry-pack, sun-dried tomatoes, shredded
150 ml/5 fl oz/2/3 cup dry red wine
4 spring onions (scallions), trimmed and finely chopped
75 g/2 3/4 oz/1 1/2 cups cooked red rice
2 tbsp freshly grated Parmesan cheese
4 thick slices granary bread
salt and pepper
spring onion (scallion), shredded, to garnish

1 Preheat the oven to 190°C/375°F/Gas Mark 5. Peel the flat mushrooms, pull out the stalks and set aside. Finely chop the stalks and place in a saucepan.

2 Add the wild mushrooms to the pan with the tomatoes and red wine. Bring to the boil, cover and simmer gently for 2–3 minutes until just tender. Drain, reserving the cooking liquid, and place in a small bowl.

3 Stir in the spring onions (scallions) and cooked rice. Season well and spoon into the flat mushrooms, pressing the mixture down gently. Sprinkle with the grated Parmesan cheese.

4 Arrange the mushrooms in an ovenproof baking dish and pour the reserved cooking juices around them. Bake in the oven for 20–25 minutes until they are just cooked.

5 Meanwhile, preheat the grill (broiler) to hot. Trim the crusts from the bread and toast on each side until lightly browned.

6 Drain the mushrooms and place each one on to a piece of toasted bread. Garnish with spring onions (scallions) and serve.

Biryani with Caramelized Onions

Serves 4 • CALORIES PER SERVING: 365 • FAT CONTENT PER SERVING: 4.5 G

INGREDIENTS

175 g/6 oz/1 cup Basmati rice, rinsed
60 g/2 oz/$^{1}/_{3}$ cup red lentils, rinsed
1 bay leaf
6 cardamom pods, split
1 tsp ground turmeric
6 cloves
1 tsp cumin seeds
1 cinnamon stick, broken
1 onion, chopped
225 g/8 oz cauliflower, broken into small florets
1 large carrot, diced
100 g/3$^{1}/_{2}$ oz frozen peas
60 g/2 oz sultanas (golden raisins)
600 ml/1 pint/2$^{1}/_{2}$ cups fresh vegetable stock
salt and pepper
naan bread, to serve

CARAMELIZED ONIONS:
2 tsp vegetable oil
1 medium red onion, shredded
1 medium onion, shredded
2 tsp caster (superfine) sugar

1 Place the rice, lentils, bay leaf, spices, onion, cauliflower, carrot, peas and sultanas (golden raisins) in a large saucepan. Season with salt and pepper and mix well.

2 Pour in the stock, bring to the boil, cover and simmer for 15 minutes, stirring occasionally, until the rice is tender. Remove from the heat and leave to stand, covered, for 10 minutes to allow the stock to be absorbed. Discard the bay leaf, cardamom pods, cloves and cinnamon stick.

3 Meanwhile, make the caramelized onions. Heat the oil in a frying pan (skillet) and fry the onions over a medium heat for 3–4 minutes until just softened. Add the caster (superfine) sugar, raise the heat and cook, stirring, for a further 2–3 minutes until the onions are golden.

4 Gently mix the rice and vegetables and transfer to warm serving plates. Spoon over the caramelized onions and serve with plain, warmed naan bread.

Soft Pancakes with Stir-fried Vegetables & Tofu (Bean Curd)

Serves 4 • CALORIES PER SERVING: 215 • FAT CONTENT PER SERVING: 8.5 G

INGREDIENTS

1 tbsp vegetable oil
1 garlic clove, crushed
2.5 cm/1 inch piece root (fresh) ginger, grated
1 bunch spring onions (scallions), trimmed and shredded lengthwise
100 g/3 1/2 oz mangetout (snow peas), topped, tailed and shredded
225 g/8 oz tofu (bean curd), drained and cut into 1 cm/1/2 inch pieces
2 tbsp dark soy sauce, plus extra to serve
2 tbsp hoi-sin sauce, plus extra to serve
60 g/2 oz canned bamboo shoots, drained
60 g/2 oz canned water chestnuts, drained and sliced
100 g/3 1/2 oz bean sprouts
1 small red chilli, deseeded and sliced thinly
1 small bunch fresh chives
12 soft Chinese pancakes

TO SERVE:
shredded Chinese leaves
1 cucumber, sliced
strips of red chilli

1 Heat the oil in a non-stick wok or a large frying pan (skillet) and stir-fry the garlic and ginger for 1 minute. Add the spring onions (scallions), mangetout (snow peas), tofu (bean curd), soy and hoi-sin sauces. Stir-fry for 2 minutes.

2 Add the bamboo shoots, water chestnuts, bean sprouts and red chilli to the pan. Stir-fry for 2 minutes until the vegetables are tender but still have bite. Snip the chives into 2.5 cm/1 inch lengths and stir them into the mixture in the pan.

3 Heat the pancakes according to the instructions on the packet and keep warm.

4 Divide the vegetables and tofu (bean curd) among the pancakes. Roll up the pancakes and serve with the Chinese leaves.

Char-grilled Mediterranean Vegetable Kebabs (Kabobs)

Makes 8 • CALORIES PER SERVING: 65 • FAT CONTENT PER SERVING: 2.5 G

INGREDIENTS

1 large red (bell) pepper
1 large green (bell) pepper
1 large orange (bell) pepper
1 large courgette (zucchini)
4 baby aubergines (eggplants)
2 medium red onions

2 tbsp lemon juice
1 tbsp olive oil
1 garlic clove, crushed
1 tbsp chopped, fresh rosemary or 1 tsp dried rosemary

salt and pepper

TO SERVE:
cracked wheat, cooked
tomato and olive relish

1 Halve and deseed the (bell) peppers and cut into even sized pieces, about 2.5 cm/1 inch wide. Trim the courgettes (zucchini), cut in half lengthwise and slice into 2.5 cm/1 inch pieces. Place the (bell) peppers and courgettes (zucchini) into a large bowl and set aside.

2 Trim the aubergines (eggplants) and quarter them lengthwise. Peel the onions, then cut each one into 8 even-sized wedges. Add the aubergine (eggplants) and onions to the bowl containing the (bell) peppers and courgettes (zucchini).

3 In a small bowl, mix together the lemon juice, olive oil, garlic, rosemary and seasoning. Pour the mixture over the vegetables and stir to coat.

4 Preheat the grill (broiler) to medium. Thread the vegetables on to 8 skewers. Arrange the kebabs (kabobs) on the rack and cook for 10–12 minutes, turning frequently until the vegetables are lightly charred and just softened.

5 Drain the vegetable kebabs (kabobs) and serve on a bed of cracked wheat accompanied with a tomato and olive relish, if wished.

1

2

4

Stuffed Vegetables Middle Eastern-style

Serves 4 • Calories per serving: 330 • Fat content per serving: 5.5 g

INGREDIENTS

4 large beefsteak tomatoes
4 medium courgettes (zucchini)
2 orange (bell) peppers
salt and pepper
warm pitta bread and low-fat hummus, to serve

FILLING:
225 g/8 oz/1 1/4 cups cracked wheat
1/4 cucumber
1 medium red onion
2 tbsp lemon juice
2 tbsp chopped fresh coriander (cilantro)
2 tbsp chopped fresh mint
1 tbsp olive oil
2 tsp cumin seeds

1 Preheat the oven to 200°C/400°F/Gas Mark 6. Cut off the tops of the tomatoes and reserve. Scoop out the tomato pulp, chop and place in a bowl. Season the tomato shells, then turn them upside down on kitchen paper.

2 Trim the courgettes (zucchini) and cut a V-shaped groove lengthwise down each one. Finely chop the cut-out courgette (zucchini) flesh and add to the tomato pulp. Season the courgette (zucchini) shells and set aside.

3 Halve the (bell) peppers. Leaving the stalks intact, cut out the seeds and discard. Season the (bell) pepper shells.

4 To make the filling, soak the cracked wheat according to the instructions on the packet. Finely chop the cucumber and add to the reserved tomato pulp and courgette (zucchini) mixture.

5 Finely chop the red onion, and add to the vegetable mixture with the lemon juice, herbs, olive oil, cumin and seasoning and mix together well.

6 Mix the wheat with the vegetables and stuff into the tomato, courgette (zucchini) and (bell) pepper shells. Place the tops on the tomatoes, transfer to a roasting tin (pan) and bake for 20–25 minutes until cooked through. Drain and serve.

Fragrant Asparagus & Orange Risotto

Serves 4–6 • CALORIES PER SERVING: 420–280 • FAT CONTENT PER SERVING: 7.5–5 G

INGREDIENTS

115 g/4 oz fine asparagus spears, trimmed
1.2 litres/2 pints/5 cups vegetable stock
2 bulbs fennel
25 g/1 oz low-fat spread
1 tsp olive oil
2 sticks celery, trimmed and chopped
2 medium leeks, trimmed and shredded
350 g/12 oz/2 cups arborio rice
3 medium oranges
salt and pepper

1 Bring a small saucepan of water to the boil and cook the asparagus for 1 minute. Drain and set aside until required.

2 Pour the stock into a saucepan and bring to the boil. Reduce the heat to maintain a gentle simmer.

3 Meanwhile, trim the fennel, reserving the fronds, and cut into thin slices. Carefully melt the low-fat spread with the oil in a large saucepan, taking care that the water in the low-fat spread does not evaporate, and gently fry the fennel, celery and leeks for 3–4 minutes until just softened. Add the rice and cook, stirring, for a further 2 minutes until mixed.

4 Add a ladleful of stock to the pan and cook gently, stirring, until absorbed. Continue ladling the stock into the rice until the rice becomes creamy, thick and tender. This process will take about 25 minutes and shouldn't be hurried.

5 Finely grate the rind and extract the juice from 1 orange and mix in to the rice. Carefully remove the peel and pith from the remaining oranges. Holding the fruit over the saucepan, cut out the orange segments and add to the rice, along with any juice that falls.

6 Stir the orange into the rice along with the asparagus spears. Season with salt and pepper, garnish with the reserved fennel fronds, and serve.

Spicy Black-Eyed Beans

Serves 4 • CALORIES PER SERVING: 445 • FAT CONTENT PER SERVING: 6 G

INGREDIENTS

- 350 g/12 oz/2 cups black-eyed beans, soaked overnight in cold water
- 1 tbsp vegetable oil
- 2 medium onions, chopped
- 1 tbsp clear honey
- 2 tbsp treacle (molasses)
- 4 tbsp dark soy sauce
- 1 tsp dry mustard powder
- 4 tbsp tomato purée (paste)
- 450 ml/16 fl oz/2 cups fresh vegetable stock
- 1 bay leaf
- 1 sprig each of rosemary, thyme and sage
- 1 small orange
- 1 tbsp cornflour (cornstarch)
- 2 medium red (bell) peppers, deseeded and diced
- pepper
- 2 tbsp chopped fresh flat-leaf parsley, to garnish
- crusty bread, to serve

1 Preheat the oven to 150°C/300°F/Gas Mark 2. Rinse the beans and place in a saucepan. Cover with water, bring to the boil and boil rapidly for 10 minutes. Drain and place in an ovenproof casserole dish.

2 Meanwhile, heat the oil in a frying pan (skillet) and fry the onions for 5 minutes. Stir in the honey, treacle (molasses), soy sauce, mustard and tomato purée (paste). Pour in the stock, bring to the boil and pour the mixture over the beans.

3 Tie the bay leaf, rosemary, thyme and sage together with a clean piece of string and add to the pan containing the beans. Using a vegetable peeler, pare off 3 pieces of orange rind and mix into the beans, along with plenty of pepper. Cover and bake for 1 hour.

4 Extract the juice from the orange and blend with the cornflour (cornstarch) to form a paste. Stir into the beans along with the red (bell) peppers. Cover and cook for 1 hour, until the sauce is rich and thick and the beans are tender. Discard the herbs and orange rind.

5 Garnish with chopped fresh flat-leaf parsley and serve with fresh crusty bread.

Mexican-style Pizzas

Serves 4 • CALORIES PER SERVING: 585 • FAT CONTENT PER SERVING: 16 G

INGREDIENTS

4 x ready-made individual pizza bases
1 tbsp olive oil
200 g/7 oz can chopped tomatoes with garlic and herbs
2 tbsp tomato purée (paste)
200 g/7 oz can kidney beans, drained and rinsed
115 g/4 oz sweetcorn kernels, thawed if frozen
1–2 tsp chilli sauce
1 large red onion, shredded
100 g/3 1/2 oz reduced-fat Cheddar cheese, grated
1 large green chilli, sliced into rings
salt and pepper

1 Preheat the oven to 220°C/425°F/Gas Mark 7. Arrange the pizza bases on a baking sheet (cookie sheet) and brush them lightly with the oil.

2 In a bowl, mix together the chopped tomatoes, tomato purée (paste), kidney beans and sweetcorn, and add chilli sauce to taste. Season with salt and pepper.

3 Spread the tomato and kidney bean mixture evenly over each pizza base to cover. Top each pizza with shredded onion and sprinkle with some grated cheese and a few slices of green chilli to taste. Bake in the oven for about 20 minutes until the vegetables are tender, the cheese has melted and the base is crisp and golden.

4 Remove the pizzas from the baking sheet (cookie sheet) and transfer to serving plates. Serve immediately.

COOK'S TIP

For a low-fat Mexican-style salad to serve with this pizza, arrange sliced tomatoes, fresh coriander (cilantro) leaves and a few slices of a small, ripe avocado. Sprinkle with fresh lime juice and coarse sea salt. Avocados have quite a high oil content, so eat in moderation.

1

3

3

Aubergine (Eggplant) Pasta Cake

Serves 6–8 • CALORIES PER SERVING: 290–215 • FAT CONTENT PER SERVING: 7–5 G

INGREDIENTS

1 medium aubergine (eggplant)
300 g/10 1/2 oz tricolour pasta shapes
115 g/4 oz low-fat soft cheese with garlic and herbs
350ml/12 fl oz/1 1/3 cups passata (sieved tomatoes)
4 tbsp grated Parmesan cheese
1 1/2 tsp dried oregano
2 tbsp dry white breadcrumbs
salt and pepper

1 Preheat the oven to 190°C/375°F/Gas Mark 5. Grease and line a 20.5 cm/8 inch round spring-form cake tin (pan).

2 Trim the aubergine (eggplant) and cut lengthwise into slices about 5 mm/¼ inch thick. Place in a bowl, sprinkle with salt, and set aside for 30 minutes to remove any bitter juices. Rinse well and drain.

3 Bring a saucepan of water to the boil and blanch the aubergine (eggplant) slices for 1 minute. Drain and pat dry using absorbent kitchen paper. Set aside.

4 Cook the pasta shapes according to the instructions on the packet; for best results, the pasta should be slightly undercooked. Drain well and return to the pan. Add the soft cheese and allow it to melt over the pasta.

5 Stir in the passata (sieved tomatoes), Parmesan cheese, oregano and seasoning. Set aside.

6 Arrange the aubergine (eggplant) over the base and sides of the tin (pan), overlapping the slices so that there are no gaps.

7 Pile the pasta mixture into the tin (pan), packing down well, and sprinkle with breadcrumbs. Bake for 20 minutes and let stand for 15 minutes.

8 Loosen the cake round the edge with a palette knife (spatula) and release from the tin. Turn out aubergine (eggplant) side uppermost and serve hot.

2

6

7

Mushroom Cannelloni

Serves 4 • CALORIES PER SERVING: 315 • FAT CONTENT PER SERVING: 3.5 G

INGREDIENTS

350 g/12 oz chestnut mushrooms, chopped finely
1 medium onion, chopped finely
1 garlic clove, crushed
1 tbsp chopped fresh thyme
1/2 tsp ground nutmeg
4 tbsp dry white wine
4 tbsp fresh white breadcrumbs
12 dried 'quick-cook' cannelloni
salt and pepper
Parmesan cheese shavings, to garnish (optional)

TOMATO SAUCE:
1 large red (bell) pepper
200 ml/7 fl oz/3/4 cup dry white wine
450 ml/16 fl oz/2 cups passata (sieved tomatoes)
2 tbsp tomato purée (paste)
2 bay leaves
1 tsp caster (superfine) sugar

1 Preheat the oven to 200°C/400°F/Gas Mark 6. Place the mushrooms, onion and garlic in a pan. Stir in the thyme, nutmeg and 4 tbsp wine. Bring to the boil, cover and simmer for 10 minutes. Stir in the breadcrumbs to bind the mixture together and season. Cool for 10 minutes.

2 Preheat the grill (broiler) to hot. To make the sauce, halve and deseed the (bell) pepper, place on the grill (broiler) rack and cook for 8–10 minutes until charred. Let cool for 10 minutes.

3 Once the (bell) pepper has cooled, peel off the skin. Chop the flesh and place in a food processor with the wine. Blend until smooth; pour into a pan.

4 Mix the remaining sauce ingredients with the (bell) pepper and wine and season. Bring to the boil and simmer for 10 minutes. Discard the bay leaves.

5 Cover the base of an ovenproof dish with a thin layer of sauce. Fill the cannelloni with the mushroom mixture and place in the dish. Spoon over the remaining sauce, cover with foil and bake for 35–40 minutes. Serve hot.

Tofu (Bean Curd) & Chickpea Burgers

Serves 4 • CALORIES PER SERVING: 280 • FAT CONTENT PER SERVING: 9 G

INGREDIENTS

1 small red onion, chopped finely
1 garlic clove, crushed
1 tsp ground cumin
1 tsp ground coriander
2 tbsp lemon juice
425 g/15 oz can chick-peas (garbanzo beans), drained and rinsed
75 g/3 oz soft silken tofu (bean curd), drained
115 g/4 oz cooked potato, diced
4 tbsp freshly chopped coriander (cilantro)
75 g/2$^{3}/_{4}$ oz dry brown breadcrumbs
1 tbsp vegetable oil
4 burger buns, split in half
2 medium tomatoes, sliced
1 large carrot, grated
salt and pepper

RELISH:
1 tsp tahini (sesame seed) paste
4 tbsp low-fat natural fromage frais (unsweetened yogurt)
2.5 cm/1 inch piece cucumber, finely chopped
1 tbsp chopped, fresh coriander (cilantro)
garlic salt, to season

1 Place the onion, garlic, spices and lemon juice in a pan, bring to the boil, cover and simmer for 5 minutes until softened.

2 Place the chick-peas (garbanzo beans), tofu (bean curd) and potato in a bowl and mash well. Stir in the onion mixture, coriander (cilantro) and seasoning, and mix. Divide into 4 equal portions and form into patties 10 cm/4 inch across.

3 Sprinkle the breadcrumbs on to a plate and press the burgers into the crumbs to coat.

4 Heat the oil in a non-stick frying pan (skillet) and fry the burgers for 5 minutes on each side until cooked and golden. Drain on kitchen paper.

5 Mix all of the relish ingredients together in a bowl and leave to chill.

6 Line the bottom half of the buns with tomato and carrot and top each with a burger. Spoon the relish over the burger and place the top half of the bun on top.

Sweet Potato & Leek Patties

Serves 4 • CALORIES PER SERVING: 385 • FAT CONTENT PER SERVING: 6.5 G

INGREDIENTS

900 g/2 lb sweet potato
4 tsp sunflower oil
2 medium leeks, chopped
1 garlic clove, crushed
2.5 cm/1 inch piece root ginger, finely chopped
200 g/7 oz can sweetcorn, drained
2 tbsp low-fat natural fromage frais (unsweetened yogurt)
60 g/2 oz wholemeal flour
salt and pepper

GINGER SAUCE:
2 tbsp white wine vinegar
2 tsp caster (superfine) sugar
1 red chilli, deseeded and chopped
2.5 cm/1 inch piece root (fresh) ginger, cut into thin strips
2 tbsp ginger wine
4 tbsp fresh vegetable stock
1 tsp cornflour (cornstarch)

TO SERVE:
lettuce leaves
spring onions (scallions), shredded

1 Peel the potatoes and cut into 2 cm/¾ inch thick pieces. Place in a pan, cover with water and boil for 10–15 minutes. Drain and mash. Leave to cool.

2 Heat 2 tsp of oil and fry the leeks, garlic and ginger for 2–3 minutes. Stir the leek mixture into the potato with the sweetcorn, seasoning and fromage frais (yogurt). Form into 8 patties and toss in flour to coat. Chill for 30 minutes.

3 Preheat the grill (broiler) to medium. Place the patties on a grill (broiler) rack and brush with oil. Grill (broil) for 5 minutes, then turn, oil and grill (broil) for another 5 minutes, or until golden. Drain on kitchen paper.

4 For the sauce, place the vinegar, sugar, chilli and ginger in a pan. Bring to the boil and simmer for 5 minutes. Stir in the ginger wine. Blend the stock and cornflour (cornstarch) to form a paste and stir into the sauce. Heat through, stirring, until thickened. Transfer the patties to serving plates, spoon over the sauce and serve.

1

2

2

Ratatouille Vegetable Grill

Serves 4 • CALORIES PER SERVING: 330 • FAT CONTENT PER SERVING: 4 G

INGREDIENTS

2 medium onions
1 garlic clove
1 medium red (bell) pepper
1 medium green (bell) pepper
1 medium aubergine (eggplant)
2 medium courgettes (zucchini)
2 x 400 g/14 oz cans chopped tomatoes
1 bouquet garni
2 tbsp tomato purée (paste)
900 g/2 lb potatoes
75 g/$2\frac{3}{4}$ oz reduced-fat Cheddar cheese, grated
salt and pepper
2 tbsp snipped fresh chives, to garnish

1 Peel and finely chop the onions and garlic. Rinse, deseed and slice the (bell) peppers. Rinse, trim and cut the aubergine (eggplant) into small dice. Rinse, trim and thinly slice the courgettes (zucchini).

2 Place the onion, garlic and (bell) peppers into a pan. Add the tomatoes, and stir in the bouquet garni, tomato purée (paste) and salt and pepper to taste. Bring to the boil, cover and simmer for 10 minutes, stirring half-way through.

3 Stir in the aubergine (eggplant) and courgettes (zucchini) and cook, uncovered, for 10 minutes, stirring.

4 Peel the potatoes and cut into 2.5 cm/1 inch cubes. Place the potatoes into another saucepan and cover with water. Bring to the boil and cook for 10–12 minutes until tender. Drain thoroughly and set aside until required.

5 Transfer the vegetables to a heatproof gratin dish. Arrange the cooked potato cubes evenly over the vegetables.

6 Preheat the grill (broiler) to medium. Sprinkle grated cheese over the potatoes and place under the grill (broiler) for 5 minutes until golden, bubbling and hot. Serve garnished with freshly snipped chives.

Mussel & Red (Bell) Pepper Salad

Serves 4 • CALORIES PER SERVING: 175 • FAT CONTENT PER SERVING: 6 G

INGREDIENTS

2 large red (bell) peppers
350 g/12 oz cooked shelled mussels, thawed if frozen
1 head of radicchio
25 g/1 oz rocket (arugula) leaves
8 cooked New Zealand mussels in their shells

TO SERVE:
lemon wedges
crusty bread

DRESSING:
1 tbsp olive oil
1 tbsp lemon juice
1 tsp finely grated lemon rind
2 tsp clear honey
1 tsp French mustard
1 tbsp snipped fresh chives
salt and pepper

1 Preheat the grill (broiler) to hot. Halve and deseed the (bell) peppers and place them skin-side up on the rack. Cook for 8–10 minutes until the skin is charred and blistered and the flesh is soft. Cool for 10 minutes, then peel off the skin.

2 Slice the (bell) pepper flesh into thin strips and place in a bowl. Gently mix in the shelled mussels and set aside.

3 To make the dressing, mix all of the ingredients until well blended. Mix into the (bell) pepper and mussel mixture until coated.

4 Remove the central core of the radicchio and shred the leaves. Place in a serving bowl with the rocket (arugula) leaves and toss together.

5 Spoon the mussel mixture into the centre of the leaves and arrange the large New Zealand mussels round the edge of the dish. Serve with lemon wedges and crusty bread.

VARIATION

Replace the shelled mussels with peeled prawns (shrimp) and the New Zealand mussels with large crevettes, if you prefer. Lime could be used instead of lemon for a different citrus flavour.

1

2

4

Sweet & Sour Fish Salad

Serves 4 • CALORIES PER SERVING: 190 • FAT CONTENT PER SERVING: 7 G

INGREDIENTS

225 g/8 oz trout fillets
225 g/8 oz white fish fillets (such as haddock or cod)
300 ml/$^1/_2$ pint/1$^1/_4$ cups water
1 stalk lemon grass
2 lime leaves
1 large red chilli
1 bunch spring onions (scallions), trimmed and shredded
115 g/4 oz fresh pineapple flesh, diced
1 small red (bell) pepper, deseeded and diced
1 bunch watercress, washed and trimmed
fresh snipped chives, to garnish

DRESSING:
1 tbsp sunflower oil
1 tbsp rice wine vinegar
pinch of chilli powder
1 tsp clear honey
salt and pepper

1 Rinse the fish, place in a frying pan (skillet) and pour over the water. Bend the lemon grass in half to bruise it and add to the pan with the lime leaves. Prick the chilli with a fork and add to the pan. Bring to the boil and simmer for 7–8 minutes. Let cool.

2 Drain the fish fillets, discarding the lemon grass, lime leaves and chilli. Flake the flesh away from the skin of the fish and place in a bowl. Gently stir in the spring onions (scallions), pineapple and (bell) pepper.

3 Arrange the washed watercress on 4 serving plates, spoon the cooked fish mixture on top and set aside.

4 To make the dressing, mix all the ingredients together and season well. Spoon over the fish and serve garnished with chives.

VARIATION

This recipe also works very well if you replace the fish with 350 g/12 oz white crab meat. Add a dash of Tabasco sauce if you like it hot!

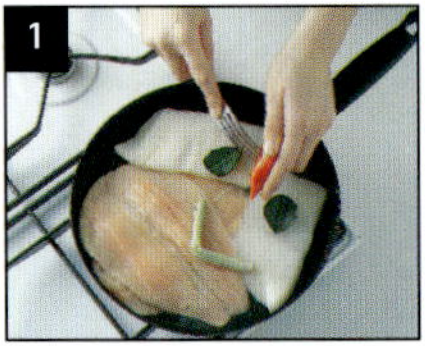

Beef & Peanut Salad

Serves 4 • CALORIES PER SERVING: 320 • FAT CONTENT PER SERVING: 14 G

INGREDIENTS

1/2 head Chinese leaves
1 large carrot
115 g/4 oz radishes
100 g/3 1/2 oz baby corn cobs
1 tbsp ground nut oil
1 red chilli, deseeded and chopped finely
1 clove garlic, chopped finely
350 g/12 oz lean beef (such as fillet, sirloin or rump), trimmed and shredded finely
1 tbsp dark soy sauce
25 g/1 oz fresh peanuts (optional)
red chilli, sliced, to garnish

DRESSING:
1 tbsp smooth peanut butter
1 tsp caster (superfine) sugar
2 tbsp light soy sauce
1 tbsp sherry vinegar
salt and pepper

1 Finely shred the Chinese leaves and arrange on a platter. Peel the carrot and cut into thin, matchstick-like strips. Wash, trim and quarter the radishes, and halve the baby corn cobs lengthwise. Arrange these ingredients around the edge of the dish and set aside.

2 Heat the oil in a non-stick wok or large frying pan (skillet) and stir-fry the chilli, garlic and beef for 5 minutes. Add the dark soy sauce and stir-fry for a further 1–2 minutes until tender and cooked through.

3 Meanwhile, make the dressing. Place all of the ingredients in a small bowl and blend them together until smooth.

4 Place the hot cooked beef in the centre of the salad ingredients. Spoon over the dressing and sprinkle with a few peanuts, if using. Garnish with slices of red chilli and serve immediately.

VARIATION

If preferred, use chicken, turkey, lean pork or even strips of venison instead of beef in this recipe. Cut off all visible fat before you begin.

Chicken & Spinach Salad

Serves 4 • CALORIES PER SERVING: 225 • FAT CONTENT PER SERVING: 6 G

INGREDIENTS

4 boneless, skinless chicken breasts, 150 g/5$^1/_2$ oz each
450 ml/16 fl oz/2 cups fresh chicken stock
1 bay leaf
225 g/8 oz fresh young spinach leaves
1 small red onion, shredded
115 g/4 oz fresh raspberries
salt and freshly ground pink peppercorns
fresh toasted croûtons, to garnish

DRESSING:
4 tbsp low-fat natural (unsweetened) yogurt
1 tbsp raspberry vinegar
2 tsp clear honey

1 Place the chicken breasts in a frying pan (skillet). Pour over the fresh chicken stock and add the bay leaf. Bring to the boil, cover and simmer for 15–20 minutes, turning half-way through, until the chicken is cooked through. Leave the chicken to cool in the liquid.

2 Arrange the spinach leaves on 4 serving plates and top with the onion. Cover and leave to chill.

3 Drain the cooked chicken and pat dry on absorbent kitchen paper. Slice the chicken breasts thinly and arrange, fanned out, over the spinach and onion. Sprinkle with the raspberries.

4 To make the dressing, mix all the ingredients together in a small bowl.

5 Drizzle a spoonful of dressing over each chicken breast and season with salt and ground pink peppercorns to taste. Serve with freshly toasted croûtons.

VARIATION

This recipe is delicious with smoked chicken, but it will be more expensive and richer, so use slightly less. It would make an impressive starter for a dinner party.

1

2

3

Pasta Provençale

Serves 4 • CALORIES PER SERVING: 295 • FAT CONTENT PER SERVING: 6 G

INGREDIENTS

225 g/8 oz penne (quills)
1 tbsp olive oil
25 g/1 oz pitted black olives, drained and chopped
25 g/1 oz dry-pack sun-dried tomatoes, soaked, drained and chopped
400 g/14 oz can artichoke hearts, drained and halved
115 g/4 oz baby courgettes (zucchini), trimmed and sliced
115 g/4 oz baby plum tomatoes, halved
100 g/3½ oz assorted baby salad leaves
salt and pepper
shredded basil leaves, to garnish

DRESSING:
4 tbsp passata (sieved tomatoes)
2 tbsp low-fat natural fromage frais (unsweetened yogurt)
1 tbsp unsweetened orange juice
1 small bunch fresh basil, shredded

1 Cook the penne (quills) according to the instructions on the packet. Do not overcook the pasta – it should still have 'bite'. Drain well and return to the pan. Stir in the olive oil, salt and pepper, olives and sun-dried tomatoes. Leave to cool.

2 Gently mix the artichokes, courgettes (zucchini) and plum tomatoes into the cooked pasta. Arrange the salad leaves in a serving bowl.

3 To make the dressing, mix all the ingredients together and toss into the vegetables and pasta.

4 Spoon the mixture on top of the salad leaves and garnish with shredded basil leaves.

VARIATION

For a non-vegetarian version, stir 225 g/8 oz canned tuna in brine, drained and flaked, into the pasta together with the vegetables. Other pasta shapes can be included – look out for farfalle (bows) and rotelle (spoked wheels).

Root Vegetable Salad

Serves 4 • CALORIES PER SERVING: 150 • FAT CONTENT PER SERVING: 9 G

INGREDIENTS

350 g/12 oz carrots
225 g/8 oz mooli (white radish)
115 g/4 oz radishes
350 g/12 oz celeriac
1 tbsp orange juice
2 sticks celery with leaves, washed and trimmed
100 g/3$^1/_2$ oz assorted salad leaves
25 g/1 oz chopped walnuts

DRESSING:
1 tbsp walnut oil
1 tbsp white wine vinegar
1 tsp wholegrain mustard
$^1/_2$ tsp finely grated orange rind
1 tsp celery seeds
salt and pepper

1 Using a sharp knife, peel and coarsely grate or very finely shred the carrots, mooli (white radish) and radishes. Set aside in separate bowls.

2 Using a sharp knife, peel and coarsely grate or finely shred the celeriac and mix with the orange juice.

3 Remove the celery leaves and reserve them for garnishing. Finely chop the celery sticks.

4 Divide the salad leaves among 4 serving plates and arrange the vegetables in small piles on top. Set aside while you make the dressing.

5 To make the dressing, mix the walnut oil, wine vinegar, mustard, orange rind, celery seeds and season with salt and pepper to taste. Drizzle a little over each salad. Shred the reserved celery leaves and sprinkle over the salad with the chopped walnuts.

COOK'S TIP

Also known as Chinese white radish and daikon, mooli resembles a large white parsnip. It has crisp, slightly pungent flesh, which can be eaten raw or cooked. It is a useful ingredient in stir-fries. Fresh mooli tend to have a stronger flavour than shop-bought ones.

Beetroot & Orange Rice Salad

Serves 4 • CALORIES PER SERVING: 335 • FAT CONTENT PER SERVING: 2.5 G

INGREDIENTS

225 g/8 oz/1 1/3 cups long-grain and wild rices (see Cook's Tip, below)
4 large oranges
450 g/1 lb cooked beetroot, peeled
2 heads of chicory
salt and pepper
fresh snipped chives, to garnish

DRESSING:
4 tbsp low-fat natural fromage frais (unsweetened yogurt)
1 garlic clove, crushed
1 tbsp wholegrain mustard
1/2 tsp finely grated orange rind
2 tsp clear honey

1 Cook the rices according to the instructions on the packet. Drain and set aside to cool.

2 Slice the top and bottom off each orange and remove the skin and pith. Holding the orange over a bowl to catch the juice, slice between each segment. Place the segments in a separate bowl. Cover the juice and leave to chill in the refrigerator until required.

3 Drain the beetroot if necessary and dice into cubes. Mix with the orange segments, cover and leave to chill.

4 When the rice has cooled, mix in the reserved orange juice and season with salt and pepper.

5 Line 4 serving bowls or plates with the chicory leaves. Spoon over the rice and top with the beetroot and orange segments.

6 Mix all the dressing ingredients together and spoon over the salad, or serve separately in a bowl, if preferred. Garnish with fresh snipped chives.

COOK'S TIP

Look out for boxes of ready-mixed long-grain and wild rices. Alternatively, cook 175 g/6 oz/1 cup white rice and 60 g/2 oz/1/4 cup wild rice separately.

2

3

5

Red Hot Slaw

Serves 4 • CALORIES PER SERVING: 200 • FAT CONTENT PER SERVING: 8.5 G

INGREDIENTS

1/2 small red cabbage
1 large carrot
2 red-skinned apples
1 tbsp lemon juice
1 medium red onion
100 g/3 1/2 oz reduced-fat Cheddar cheese, grated

TO GARNISH:
red chilli strips
carrot strips

DRESSING:
3 tbsp reduced-calorie mayonnaise
3 tbsp low-fat natural (unsweetened) yogurt
1 garlic clove, crushed
1 tsp paprika
1–2 tsp chilli powder
pinch cayenne pepper (optional)
salt and pepper

1 Cut the red cabbage in half and remove the central core. Finely shred the leaves and place in a large bowl. Peel and coarsely grate or finely shred the carrot and mix into the cabbage.

2 Core the apples and dice, leaving on the skins. Place in another bowl and toss in the lemon juice to prevent the apple browning. Mix the apple into the cabbage and carrot.

3 Peel and finely shred or grate the onion. Stir into the other vegetables along with the cheese and mix together.

4 To make the dressing, mix together the mayonnaise, yogurt, garlic and paprika in a small bowl. Add chilli powder according to taste, and the cayenne pepper, if using – remember this will add more spice to the dressing. Season well.

5 Toss the dressing into the vegetables and mix well. Cover and leave to chill in the refrigerator for 1 hour to allow the flavours to develop. Serve garnished with strips of red chilli and carrot.

Pasta Niçoise Salad

Serves 4 • CALORIES PER SERVING: 370 • FAT CONTENT PER SERVING: 9 G

INGREDIENTS

225 g/8 oz farfalle (bows)
175 g/6 oz French (green) beans, topped and tailed
350 g/12 oz fresh tuna steaks
115 g/4 oz baby plum tomatoes, halved
8 anchovy fillets, drained on absorbent kitchen paper
2 tbsp capers in brine, drained
25 g/1 oz pitted black olives in brine, drained
fresh basil leaves, to garnish
salt and pepper

DRESSING:
1 tbsp olive oil
1 garlic clove, crushed
1 tbsp lemon juice
1/2 tsp finely grated lemon rind
1 tbsp shredded fresh basil leaves

1 Cook the pasta in lightly salted boiling water according to the instructions on the packet until just cooked. Drain well, set aside and keep warm.

2 Bring a small saucepan of lightly salted water to the boil and cook the French (green) beans for 5–6 minutes until just tender. Drain well and toss into the pasta. Set aside and keep warm.

3 Preheat the grill (broiler) to medium. Rinse and pat the tuna steaks dry on absorbent kitchen paper. Season on both sides with black pepper. Place the tuna steaks on the grill (broiler) rack and cook for 4–5 minutes on each side until cooked through.

4 Drain the tuna on absorbent kitchen paper and flake into bite-sized pieces. Toss the tuna into the pasta along with the tomatoes, anchovies, capers and olives. Set aside and keep warm.

5 Meanwhile, prepare the dressing. Mix all the ingredients together and season with salt and pepper to taste. Pour the dressing over the pasta mixture and mix carefully. Transfer to a warmed serving bowl and serve sprinkled with fresh basil leaves.

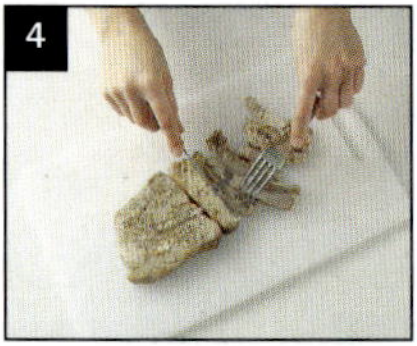

Coconut Couscous Salad

Serves 4 • CALORIES PER SERVING: 270 • FAT CONTENT PER SERVING: 10 G

INGREDIENTS

350 g/12 oz precooked couscous
175 g/6 oz no-need-to-soak dried apricots
1 small bunch fresh chives
2 tbsp unsweetened desiccated (shredded) coconut
1 tsp ground cinnamon
salt and pepper
shredded mint leaves, to garnish

DRESSING:
1 tbsp olive oil
2 tbsp unsweetened orange juice
1/2 tsp finely grated orange rind
1 tsp wholegrain mustard
1 tsp clear honey
2 tbsp chopped fresh mint leaves

1 Soak the couscous according to the instructions on the packet.

2 Bring a large saucepan of water to the boil. Transfer the couscous to a steamer or large sieve (strainer) lined with muslin (cheesecloth) and place over the pan of water. Cover and steam according to the instructions on the packet. Remove from the heat, place in a heatproof bowl and set aside to cool.

3 Meanwhile, slice the apricots into thin strips and place in a small bowl. Using scissors, snip the chives over the apricots.

4 When the couscous is cool, mix in the apricots, chives, coconut and cinnamon. Season well.

5 To make the dressing, mix all the ingredients together and season. Pour over the couscous and mix until well combined. Cover and leave to chill for 1 hour to allow the flavours to develop. Serve garnished with mint leaves.

COOK'S TIP

To serve this salad hot, when the couscous has been steamed, mix in the apricots, chives, coconut, cinnamon and seasoning along with 1 tbsp olive oil. Transfer to a warmed serving bowl and serve.

Baking & Desserts

The ideal ending to a meal is fresh fruit, topped with low-fat yogurt or fromage frais. Fruit contains no fat and is sweet enough not to need extra sugar, and it is also a valuable source of vitamins and fibre – ideal in every way for anyone who cares about their own and their family's health.

There are, however, dozens of other ways in which fruit can be used as the basis for desserts and bakes, and thanks to modern transportation systems the range of unusual and exotic fruits available in supermarkets seems to expand every week. Experiment with some of these unfamiliar fruits in delicious warm desserts, sophisticated mousses and fools, and satisfying cakes, and use old favourites in enticing new ways.

From an elegant Strawberry Roulade to add the perfect finishing touch to a dinner party to a deliciously moist Carrot & Ginger Cake to offer to unexpected guests, you will find the perfect recipe for every occasion on the following pages.

Paper-thin Fruit Pies

Serves 4 • CALORIES PER SERVING: 185 • FAT CONTENT: 7.5 G

INGREDIENTS

1 medium eating (dessert) apple
1 medium ripe pear
2 tbsp lemon juice
60 g/2 oz low-fat spread
4 rectangular sheets of filo pastry, thawed if frozen
2 tbsp low-sugar apricot jam
1 tbsp unsweetened orange juice
2 tsp icing (confectioner's) sugar, for dusting
low-fat custard, to serve

1 Preheat the oven to 200°C/400°F/Gas Mark 6. Core and thinly slice the apple and pear and toss them in the lemon juice to prevent discoloration.

2 Melt the low-fat spread over a gentle heat.

3 Cut the sheets of pastry into 4 and cover with a clean, damp tea towel (dish cloth). Brush 4 non-stick Yorkshire pudding tins (large muffin pans), measuring 10 cm/4 inch across, with a little of the low-fat spread.

4 Working on each pie separately, brush 4 sheets of pastry with the melted low-fat spread. Press a small sheet of pastry into the base of one tin (pan). Arrange the other sheets of pastry on top at slightly different angles. Repeat with the other sheets of pastry to make another 3 pies.

5 Arrange the apple and pear slices alternately in the centre of each pastry case and lightly crimp the edges of the pastry of each pie.

6 Mix the apricot jam and orange juice together until smooth and generously brush over the fruit. Bake for 12–15 minutes. Dust with icing (confectioner's) sugar and serve hot with low-fat custard.

VARIATION

Other combinations of fruit are equally delicious. Try peach and apricot, raspberry and apple, or pineapple and mango.

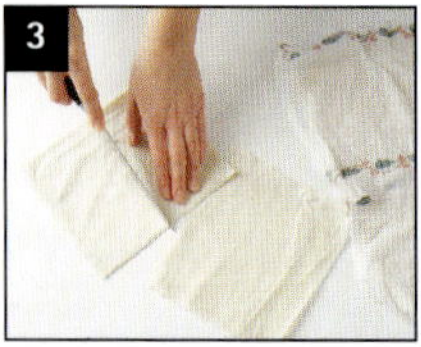

Almond Trifles

Serves 4 • CALORIES PER SERVING: 230 • FAT CONTENT PER SERVING: 3.5 G

INGREDIENTS

8 Amaretti di Saronno biscuits
4 tbsp brandy or Amaretti liqueur
225 g/8 oz raspberries
300 ml/½ pint/1¼ cups low-fat custard
300 ml/½ pint/1¼ cups low-fat natural fromage frais (unsweetened yogurt)
1 tsp almond essence (extract)
15 g/½ oz toasted almonds, flaked (slivered)
1 tsp cocoa powder

1 Place the biscuits in a mixing bowl and using the end of a rolling pin, carefully crush the biscuits into small pieces.

2 Divide the crushed biscuits among 4 serving glasses. Sprinkle the brandy or liqueur over the crushed biscuits and leave to stand for about 30 minutes to allow the biscuits to soften.

3 Top the layer of crushed biscuits with a layer of raspberries, reserving a few raspberries for decoration, and spoon over enough custard to just cover.

4 Mix the fromage frais (unsweetened yogurt) with the almond essence (extract) and spoon over the custard. Leave to chill in the refrigerator for about 30 minutes.

5 Just before serving, sprinkle over the toasted almonds and dust with cocoa powder. Decorate with the reserved raspberries and serve at once.

VARIATION

Try this trifle with assorted summer fruits. If they are a frozen mix, use them frozen and allow them to thaw so that the juices soak into the biscuit base – it will taste truly delicious.

Cheese Hearts with Strawberry Sauce

Serves 4 • CALORIES PER SERVING: 120 • FAT CONTENT PER SERVING: 0.6 G

INGREDIENTS

150 g/5½ oz low-fat cottage cheese
150 ml/5 fl oz/⅔ cup low-fat natural fromage frais (unsweetened yogurt)
1 medium egg white
2 tbsp caster (superfine) sugar
1–2 tsp vanilla essence (extract)
rose-scented geranium leaves, to decorate (optional)

SAUCE:
225 g/8 oz strawberries
4 tbsp unsweetened orange juice
2–3 tsp icing (confectioner's) sugar

1 Line 4 heart-shaped moulds (molds) with clean muslin (cheesecloth). Place a sieve (strainer) over a mixing bowl and using the back of a metal spoon, press through the cottage cheese. Mix in the fromage frais (yogurt).

2 Whisk the egg white until stiff. Fold into the cheeses, with the caster (superfine) sugar and vanilla essence (extract).

3 Place the moulds (molds) on a wire rack set over a roasting tin (pan). Spoon the the cheese mixture into the moulds (molds) and smooth over the tops. Leave to chill for 1 hour or until firm and well drained.

4 To make the sauce, wash the strawberries under cold running water. Reserving a few strawberries for decoration, hull and chop the remainder. Place the strawberries in a blender or food processor with the orange juice and process until smooth. Alternatively, push through a sieve (strainer) to purée. Mix with the icing (confectioner's) sugar to taste. Cover and leave to chill until required.

5 Remove the cheese hearts from the moulds (molds) and transfer to serving plates. Remove the muslin (cheesecloth), decorate with the reserved strawberries and geranium leaves (if using) and serve with the sauce.

1

2

3

Almond & Sultana Cheesecakes

Serves 4 • CALORIES PER SERVING: 315 • FAT CONTENT PER SERVING: 16 G

INGREDIENTS

- 12 Amaretti di Saronno biscuits
- 1 medium egg white, beaten
- 225 g/8 oz skimmed-milk soft cheese
- 1/2 tsp almond essence (extract)
- 1/2 tsp finely grated lime rind
- 25 g/1 oz ground almonds
- 25 g/1 oz caster (superfine) sugar
- 60 g/2 oz sultanas
- 2 tsp powdered gelatine
- 2 tbsp boiling water
- 2 tbsp lime juice

TO DECORATE:

- 25 g/1 oz flaked (slivered) toasted almonds
- strips of lime rind

1 Preheat the oven to 180°C/350°F/Gas Mark 4. Place the biscuits in a clean plastic bag, seal the bag and using a rolling pin, crush them into small pieces. Place the crumbs in a bowl and bind together with the egg white.

2 Arrange 4 non-stick pastry rings or poached egg rings, 9 cm/3½ inches across, on a baking sheet (cookie sheet) lined with baking parchment. Divide the biscuit mixture into 4 equal portions and spoon it into the rings, pressing down well. Bake for 10 minutes until crisp and leave to cool in the rings.

3 Beat together the soft cheese, almond essence (extract), lime rind, ground almonds, sugar and sultanas until well mixed.

4 Dissolve the gelatine in the boiling water and stir in the lime juice. Fold into the cheese mixture and spoon over the biscuit bases. Smooth over the tops and chill for 1 hour until set.

5 Loosen the cheesecakes using a small palette knife (spatula) and transfer to serving plates. Decorate with toasted almonds and lime rind, and serve.

VARIATION

If you prefer, substitute chopped no-need-to-soak dried apricots for the sultanas.

1

2

4

Red Fruits with Foaming Sauce

Serves 4 • CALORIES PER SERVING: 220 • FAT CONTENT PER SERVING: 0.3 G

INGREDIENTS

225 g/8 oz redcurrants, washed and trimmed, thawed if frozen
225 g/8 oz cranberries
75 g/3 oz light muscovado sugar
200 ml/7 fl oz/$^3/_4$ cup unsweetened apple juice
1 cinnamon stick, broken
300 g/10$^1/_2$ oz small strawberries, washed, hulled and halved

SAUCE:
225 g/8 oz raspberries, thawed if frozen
2 tbsp fruit cordial
100 g/3$^1/_2$ oz marshmallows

1 Place the redcurrants, cranberries and sugar in a saucepan. Pour in the apple juice and add the cinnamon stick. Bring the mixture to the boil and simmer gently for 10 minutes until the fruit has just softened.

2 Stir the strawberries into the cranberry and sugar mixture and mix well. Transfer the mixture to a bowl, cover and leave to chill for about 1 hour. Remove and discard the cinnamon stick.

3 Just before serving, make the sauce. Place the raspberries and fruit cordial in a small pan, bring to the boil and simmer for 2–3 minutes until the fruit is just beginning to soften. Stir the marshmallows into the raspberry mixture and heat through, stirring, until the marshmallows begin to melt.

4 Transfer the fruit salad to serving bowls. Spoon over the raspberry and marshmallow sauce and serve.

VARIATION

This sauce is delicious poured over low-fat ice cream. For an extra-colourful sauce, replace the raspberries with an assortment of summer berries.

Brown Bread Ice Cream

Serves 4 • CALORIES PER SERVING: 265 • FAT CONTENT PER SERVING: 6 G

INGREDIENTS

175 g/6 oz fresh wholemeal breadcrumbs
25 g/1 oz finely chopped walnuts
60 g/2 oz caster (superfine) sugar
1/2 tsp ground nutmeg
1 tsp finely grated orange rind
450 ml/16 fl oz/2 cups low-fat natural (unsweetened) yogurt
2 large egg whites

TO DECORATE:
walnut halves
orange slices
fresh mint leaves

1 Preheat the grill (broiler) to medium. Mix the breadcrumbs, walnuts and sugar together and spread over a sheet of foil in the grill (broiler) pan. Grill (broil), stirring frequently, for 5 minutes until crisp and evenly browned. (Take care that the sugar does not burn.) Remove from the heat and leave to cool.

2 When cool, transfer to a mixing bowl and mix in the nutmeg, orange rind and yogurt. In another bowl, whisk the egg whites until stiff. Gently fold into the breadcrumb mixture, using a metal spoon.

3 Spoon the mixture into 4 mini-basins, smooth over the tops and freeze for 1½–2 hours until firm.

4 To serve, hold the bases of the moulds (molds) in hot water for a few seconds, then turn out on to serving plates. Serve immediately, decorated with walnut halves, orange slices and fresh mint leaves.

COOK'S TIP

If you don't have mini-basins, use ramekins or teacups or, if you prefer, use one large bowl. Alternatively, spoon the mixture into a large, freezing container to freeze and serve the ice cream in scoops.

1

2

3

Chocolate Cheese Pots

Serves 4 • CALORIES PER SERVING: 170 • FAT CONTENT PER SERVING: 3 G

INGREDIENTS

300 ml/$^1/_2$ pint/1$^1/_4$ cups low-fat natural fromage frais (unsweetened yogurt)
150 ml/5 fl oz/$^2/_3$ cup low-fat natural (unsweetened) yogurt
25 g/1 oz icing (confectioner's) sugar
4 tsp low-fat drinking chocolate powder
4 tsp cocoa powder
1 tsp vanilla essence (extract)
2 tbsp dark rum (optional)
2 medium egg whites
4 chocolate cake decorations

TO SERVE:
pieces of kiwi fruit, orange and banana
strawberries and raspberries

1 Combine the fromage frais (unsweetened yogurt) and low-fat yogurt in a mixing bowl. Sift in the sugar, drinking chocolate and cocoa powder and mix well. Add the vanilla essence (extract) and rum, if using.

2 In another bowl, whisk the egg whites until stiff. Using a metal spoon, fold the egg whites into the fromage frais (unsweetened yogurt) and chocolate mixture.

3 Spoon the fromage frais (unsweetened yogurt) and chocolate mixture into 4 small china dessert pots and leave to chill for about 30 minutes. Decorate each chocolate cheese pot with a chocolate cake decoration.

4 Serve each chocolate cheese pot with an assortment of fresh fruit, such as pieces of kiwi fruit, orange and banana, and a few whole strawberries and raspberries.

VARIATION

This chocolate mixture would make an excellent filling for a cheesecake. Make the base out of crushed Amaretti di Saronno biscuits and egg white, and set the filling with 2 tsp powdered gelatine dissolved in 2 tbsp boiling water. Make sure you use biscuits made from apricot kernels, which are virtually fat free.

Citrus Meringue Crush

Serves 4 • CALORIES PER SERVING: 195 • FAT CONTENT PER SERVING: 0.6 G

INGREDIENTS

8 ready-made meringue nests
300 ml/½ pint/1¼ cups low-fat natural (unsweetened) yogurt
½ tsp finely grated orange rind
½ tsp finely grated lemon rind
½ tsp finely grated lime rind
2 tbsp orange liqueur or unsweetened orange juice

TO DECORATE:
sliced kumquat
lime rind, grated

SAUCE:
60 g/2 oz kumquats
8 tbsp unsweetened orange juice
2 tbsp lemon juice
2 tbsp lime juice
2 tbsp water
2–3 tsp caster (superfine) sugar
1 tsp cornflour (cornstarch) mixed with 1 tbsp water

1 Place the meringues in a clean plastic bag, seal the bag and using a rolling pin, crush the meringues into small pieces. Transfer to a mixing bowl.

2 Stir the yogurt, grated citrus rinds and the liqueur or juice into the crushed meringue. Spoon the mixture into 4 mini-basins, smooth over the tops and freeze for 1½–2 hours until firm.

3 To make the sauce, thinly slice the kumquats and place them in a small pan with the fruit juices and water. Bring gently to the boil and then simmer over a low heat for 3–4 minutes until the kumquats have just softened.

4 Sweeten with sugar to taste, stir in the cornflour (cornstarch) mixture and cook, stirring, until thickened. Pour into a small bowl, cover the surface with a layer of cling film (plastic wrap) and leave to cool – the film will help prevent a skin forming. Leave to chill.

5 To serve, dip the meringue basins in hot water for 5 seconds or until they loosen, and turn on to serving plates. Spoon over a little sauce, decorate with slices of kumquat and lime rind and serve immediately.

1

2

3

Tropical Fruit Fool

Serves 4 • CALORIES PER SERVING: 170 • FAT CONTENT PER SERVING: 0.6 G

INGREDIENTS

1 medium ripe mango
2 kiwi fruit
1 medium banana
2 tbsp lime juice
1/2 tsp finely grated lime rind, plus extra to decorate
2 medium egg whites
425 g/15 oz can low-fat custard
1/2 tsp vanilla essence (extract)
2 passion fruit

1 To peel the mango, slice either side of the smooth, flat central stone. Roughly chop the flesh and blend the fruit in a food processor or blender until smooth. Alternatively, mash the chopped mango flesh with a fork.

2 Peel the kiwi fruit, chop the flesh into small pieces and place in a bowl. Peel and chop the banana and add to the bowl. Toss all of the fruit in the lime juice and rind and mix well to prevent discoloration.

3 In a grease-free bowl, whisk the egg whites until stiff and then gently fold in the custard and vanilla essence (extract) until thoroughly mixed.

4 In 4 tall glasses, alternately layer the chopped fruit, mango purée and custard mixture, finishing with the custard on top. Leave to chill in the refrigerator for 20 minutes.

5 Halve the passion fruits, scoop out the seeds and spoon the passion fruit over the fruit fools.

6 Decorate each serving with the extra lime rind and serve.

VARIATION

Other tropical fruits to try include papaya purée, with chopped pineapple and dates, and tamarillo or pomegranate seeds to decorate. Or make a summer fruit fool by using strawberry purée, topped with raspberries and blackberries, with cherries to finish.

1

2

4

Brown Sugar Pavlovas

Serves 4 • CALORIES PER SERVING: 170 • FAT CONTENT PER SERVING: 0.2 G

INGREDIENTS

2 large egg whites
1 tsp cornflour (cornstarch)
1 tsp raspberry vinegar
100 g/3½ oz light muscovado sugar, crushed free of lumps
2 tbsp redcurrant jelly
2 tbsp unsweetened orange juice
150 ml/5 fl oz/¾ cup low-fat natural fromage frais (unsweetened yogurt)
175 g/6 oz raspberries, thawed if frozen
rose-scented geranium leaves, to decorate (optional)

1 Preheat the oven to 150°C/300°F/Gas Mark 2. Line a large baking sheet (cookie sheet) with baking parchment. In a large, grease-free bowl, whisk the egg whites until very stiff and dry. Fold in the cornflour (cornstarch) and vinegar.

2 Gradually whisk in the sugar, a spoonful at a time, until the mixture is thick and glossy.

3 Divide the mixture into 4 and spoon on to the baking sheet (cookie sheet), spaced well apart. Smooth each into a round, about 10 cm/4 inch across, and bake in the oven for 40–45 minutes until lightly browned and crisp; let cool.

4 Place the redcurrant jelly and orange juice in a small pan and heat, stirring, until melted. Leave to cool for 10 minutes.

5 Using a palette knife (spatula), carefully remove each pavlova from the baking parchment and transfer to a serving plate. Top with fromage frais (unsweetened yogurt) and raspberries. Spoon over the redcurrant jelly mixture to glaze. Decorate and serve.

VARIATION

Make a large pavlova by forming the meringue into a round, measuring 18 cm/ 7 inches across, on a lined baking sheet (cookie sheet) and bake for 1 hour.

1

2

3

Apricot & Orange Jellies

Serves 4 • CALORIES PER SERVING: 220 • FAT CONTENT PER SERVING: 4.5 G

INGREDIENTS

225 g/8 oz no-need-to-soak dried apricots
300 ml/½ pint/1¼ cups unsweetened orange juice
2 tbsp lemon juice
2–3 tsp clear honey
1 tbsp powdered gelatine
4 tbsp boiling water

CINNAMON 'CREAM':
115 g/4 oz medium fat ricotta cheese
1 tsp ground cinnamon
1 tbsp clear honey
115 g/4 oz low-fat natural fromage frais (unsweetened yogurt)

TO DECORATE:
orange segments
sprigs of mint

1 Place the apricots in a saucepan and pour in the orange juice. Bring to the boil, cover and simmer for 15–20 minutes until plump and soft. Leave to cool for 10 minutes.

2 Transfer the mixture to a blender or food processor and blend until smooth. Stir in the lemon juice and add the honey. Pour the mixture into a measuring jug and make up to 600 ml/1 pint /2½ cups with cold water.

3 Dissolve the gelatine in the boiling water and stir into the apricot mixture.

4 Pour the mixture into 4 individual moulds (molds), each 150 ml/5 fl oz/⅔ cup, or 1 large mould (mold), 600 ml/1 pint/2½ cups. Chill until set.

5 Meanwhile, make the cinnamon 'cream'. Mix all the ingredients together and place in a small bowl. Cover and leave to chill.

6 To turn out the jellies, dip the moulds (molds) in hot water for a few seconds to loosen and invert on to serving plates. Decorate and serve with the cinnamon 'cream' dusted with extra cinnamon.

VARIATION

Other fruits that would work well in this recipe instead of the apricots are dried peaches, mangoes and pears.

Sticky Sesame Bananas

Serves 4 • CALORIES PER SERVING: 300 • FAT CONTENT PER SERVING: 4.5 G

INGREDIENTS

4 ripe medium bananas
3 tbsp lemon juice
115 g/4 oz caster (superfine) sugar
4 tbsp cold water
2 tbsp sesame seeds
150 ml/5 fl oz/$^2/_3$ cup low-fat natural fromage frais (unsweetened yogurt)
1 tbsp icing (confectioner's) sugar
1 tsp vanilla essence (extract)
lemon and lime rind, shredded, to decorate

1 Peel the bananas and cut into 5 cm/2 inch pieces. Place the banana in a bowl, spoon over the lemon juice and stir well to coat – this will prevent the bananas from discoloring.

2 Place the sugar and water in a small pan and heat gently, stirring, until the sugar dissolves. Bring to the boil and cook for 5–6 minutes until the mixture caramelizes.

3 Drain the bananas and blot with absorbent kitchen paper to dry. Line a baking sheet (cookie sheet) or board with parchment and arrange the bananas, well spaced out, on top.

4 Drizzle the caramel over the bananas, working quickly because the caramel sets almost instantly. Sprinkle over the sesame seeds and leave to cool for 10 minutes.

5 Meanwhile, mix the fromage frais (unsweetened yogurt) with the icing (confectioner's) sugar and vanilla essence (extract).

6 Peel the bananas away from the paper and arrange on serving plates. Serve the fromage frais (unsweetened yogurt) as a dip, decorated with the lemon and lime rind.

COOK'S TIP

For best results, use a cannelle knife or a potato peeler to peel away thin strips of rind from the fruit, taking care not to include any bitter pith. Blanch the shreds in boiling water for 1 minute, then refresh in cold water.

1

3

4

Mocha Swirl Mousse

Serves 4 • CALORIES PER SERVING: 130 • FAT CONTENT PER SERVING: 6.5 G

INGREDIENTS

- 1 tbsp coffee and chicory essence (extract)
- 2 tsp cocoa powder, plus extra for dusting
- 1 tsp low-fat drinking chocolate powder
- 150 ml/5 fl oz/$^2/_3$ cup half-fat crème fraîche, plus 4 tsp to serve (see Cook's Tip, below)
- 2 tsp powdered gelatine
- 2 tbsp boiling water
- 2 large egg whites
- 2 tbsp caster (superfine) sugar
- 4 chocolate coffee beans, to serve

1 Place the coffee and chicory essence (extract) in one bowl, and 2 tsp cocoa powder and the drinking chocolate in another bowl. Divide the crème fraîche between the 2 bowls and mix both until well combined.

2 Dissolve the gelatine in the boiling water and set aside. In a grease-free bowl, whisk the egg whites and sugar until stiff and divide this mixture evenly between the coffee and chocolate mixtures.

3 Divide the dissolved gelatine between the 2 mixtures and, using a large metal spoon, gently fold until well mixed.

4 Spoon small amounts of the 2 mousses alternately into 4 serving glasses and swirl together gently. Chill for 1 hour or until set.

5 To serve, top each mousse with 1 tbsp of crème fraîche, a chocolate coffee bean and a light dusting of cocoa powder.

COOK'S TIP

Traditional crème fraîche is soured cream and has a fat content of around 40 per cent. It is thick and has a slightly sour and nutty flavour. Lower fat versions have a reduced fat content and are slightly looser in texture, but they should be used in a low-fat diet only occasionally. If you want to use a lower fat alternative, a reduced fat, unsweetened yogurt or fromage frais would be more suitable.

1

2

4

Fruit & Fibre Layers

Serves 4 • CALORIES PER SERVING: 340 • FAT CONTENT PER SERVING: 6 G

INGREDIENTS

115 g/4 oz no-need-to-soak dried apricots
115 g/4 oz no-need-to-soak dried prunes
115 g/4 oz no-need-to-soak dried peaches
60g /2 oz dried apple
25 g/1 oz dried cherries
450 ml/16 fl oz/2 cups unsweetened apple juice
6 cardamom pods
6 cloves
1 cinnamon stick, broken
300 ml/½ pint/1¼ cups low-fat natural yogurt
115 g/4 oz crunchy oat cereal
apricot slices, to decorate

1 To make the fruit compote, place the dried apricots, prunes, peaches, apples and cherries in a saucepan and pour in the apple juice.

2 Add the cardamom pods, cloves and cinnamon stick to the pan, bring to the boil and simmer for 10–15 minutes until the fruits are plump and tender.

3 Leave the mixture to cool completely in the pan. Remove and discard the spices from the fruits, then transfer the mixture to a bowl and leave to chill in the refrigerator for 1 hour.

4 Spoon the compote into 4 dessert glasses, layering it alternately with yogurt and oat cereal, finishing with the oat cereal on top.

5 Decorate each dessert with slices of apricot and serve at once.

COOK'S TIP

There are many dried fruits available, including mangoes and pears, some of which need soaking, so read the instructions on the packet before use. Also, check the ingredients label, because several types of dried fruit have added sugar or are rolled in sugar, and this will affect the sweetness of the dish that you use them in.

Pan-cooked Apples in Red Wine

Serves 4 • CALORIES PER SERVING: 200 • FAT CONTENT PER SERVING: 4.5 G

INGREDIENTS

4 eating (dessert) apples
2 tbsp lemon juice
40 g/1 1/2 oz low-fat spread
60 g/2 oz light muscovado sugar
1 small orange
1 cinnamon stick, broken
150 ml/5 fl oz/2/3 cup red wine
225 g/8 oz raspberries, hulled and thawed if frozen
sprigs of fresh mint, to decorate

1 Peel and core the apples, then cut them into thick wedges. Place the apples in a bowl and toss in the lemon juice to prevent the fruit from discoloring.

2 In a frying pan (skillet), gently melt the low-fat spread over a low heat, add the sugar and stir to form a paste.

3 Stir the apple wedges into the pan and cook, stirring occasionally, for 2 minutes until well coated in the sugar paste.

4 Using a vegetable peeler, pare off a few strips of orange rind. Add the orange rind to the pan along with the cinnamon pieces. Extract the juice from the orange and pour into the pan with the red wine. Bring to the boil, then simmer for 10 minutes, stirring.

5 Add the raspberries to the pan and cook for 5 minutes until the apples are tender.

6 Discard the orange rind and cinnamon pieces. Transfer the apple and raspberry mixture to a serving plate together with the wine sauce. Decorate with a sprig of fresh mint and serve hot.

VARIATION

For other fruity combinations, cook the apples with blackberries, blackcurrants or redcurrants. You may need to add more sugar if you use currants as they are not as sweet as raspberries.

Mixed Fruit Brûlées

Serves 4 • Calories per serving: 225 • Fat content per serving: 11 g

INGREDIENTS

450 g/1 lb prepared, assorted summer fruits (such as strawberries, raspberries, blackcurrants, redcurrants and cherries), thawed if frozen
150 ml/5 fl oz/$^3/_4$ cup half-fat double (heavy) cream alternative
150 ml/5 fl oz/$^3/_4$ cup low-fat natural fromage frais (unsweetened yogurt)
1 tsp vanilla essence (extract)
4 tbsp demerara (brown crystal) sugar

1 Divide the strawberries, raspberries, blackcurrants, redcurrants and cherries evenly among 4 small, heatproof ramekin dishes.

2 Mix together the half-fat cream alternative, fromage frais (unsweetened yogurt) and vanilla essence (extract). Generously spoon the mixture over the fruit.

3 Preheat the grill (broiler) to hot. Top each serving with 1 tablespoon demerara (brown crystal) sugar and grill (broil) the desserts for 2–3 minutes, until the sugar melts and begins to caramelize. Serve hot.

VARIATION

If you are making this dessert for a special occasion, soak the fruits in 2–3 tbsp fruit liqueur before topping with the cream mixture.

COOK'S TIP

Look out for half-fat creams, in single and double (light and heavy) varieties. They are good substitutes for occasional use. Alternatively, in this recipe, omit the cream and double the quantity of fromage frais (yogurt) for a lower fat version.

Grilled Fruit Platter with Lime 'Butter'

Serves 4 • CALORIES PER SERVING: 220 • FAT CONTENT PER SERVING: 6.5 G

INGREDIENTS

1 baby pineapple
1 ripe papaya
1 ripe mango
2 kiwi fruit
4 apple (finger) bananas
4 tbsp dark rum
1 tsp ground allspice
2 tbsp lime juice
4 tbsp dark muscovado sugar

LIME 'BUTTER':
60 g/2 oz low-fat spread
$^1/_2$ tsp finely grated lime rind
1 tbsp icing (confectioner's) sugar

1 Quarter the pineapple, trimming away most of the leaves, and place in a shallow dish. Peel the papaya, cut it in half and scoop out the seeds. Cut the flesh into thick wedges and place in the same dish as the pineapple.

2 Peel the mango, cut either side of the smooth, central flat stone and remove the stone. Slice the flesh into thick wedges. Peel the kiwi fruit and cut in half. Peel the bananas. Add all of these fruits to the dish.

3 Sprinkle over the rum, allspice and lime juice, cover and leave at room temperature for 30 minutes, turning occasionally, to allow the flavours to develop.

4 Meanwhile, make the 'butter'. Place the low-fat spread in a small bowl and beat in the lime rind and sugar until well mixed. Leave to chill in the refrigerator until required.

5 Preheat the grill (broiler) to hot. Drain the fruit, reserving the juices, and arrange in the grill (broiler) pan. Sprinkle with the sugar and grill (broil) for 3–4 minutes until hot, bubbling and just beginning to char.

6 Transfer the fruit to a serving plate and spoon over the juices. Serve with the lime 'butter'.

VARIATION

Serve with a light sauce of 300 ml/ $^1/_2$ pint/$1^1/_4$ cups tropical fruit juice thickened with 2 tsp arrowroot.

Baked Pears with Cinnamon & Brown Sugar

Serves 4 • CALORIES PER SERVING: 160 • FAT CONTENT PER SERVING: 6 G

INGREDIENTS

4 ripe pears
2 tbsp lemon juice
4 tbsp light muscovado sugar
1 tsp ground cinnamon
60 g/2 oz low-fat spread
low-fat custard, to serve
lemon rind, finely grated, to decorate

1 Preheat the oven to 200°C/400°F/Gas Mark 6. Core and peel the pears, then slice them in half lengthwise and brush all over with the lemon juice to prevent the pears from discoloring. Place the pears, cored side down, in a small non-stick roasting tin (pan).

2 Place the sugar, cinnamon and low-fat spread in a small saucepan and heat gently, stirring, until the sugar has melted. Keep the heat low to stop too much water evaporating from the low-fat spread as it gets hot. Spoon the mixture over the pears.

3 Bake for 20–25 minutes or until the pears are tender and golden, occasionally spooning the sugar mixture over the fruit during the cooking time.

4 To serve, heat the custard until it is piping hot and spoon over the bases of 4 warm dessert plates. Arrange 2 pear halves on each plate. Decorate with grated lemon rind and serve.

VARIATION

This recipe also works well if you use cooking apples. For alternative flavours, replace the cinnamon with ground ginger and serve the pears sprinkled with chopped stem ginger in syrup. Alternatively, use ground allspice and spoon over some warmed dark rum to serve.

1

2

2

Baked Apples with Blackberries

Serves 4 • Calories per serving: 250 • Fat content per serving: 2 g

INGREDIENTS

4 medium-sized cooking apples
1 tbsp lemon juice
100 g/3 1/2 oz prepared blackberries, thawed if frozen
15 g/1/2 oz flaked (slivered) almonds
1/2 tsp ground allspice
1/2 tsp finely grated lemon rind
2 tbsp demerara (brown crystal) sugar
300 ml/1/2 pint/1 1/4 cups ruby port
1 cinnamon stick, broken
2 tsp cornflour (cornstarch) blended with 2 tbsp cold water
low-fat custard, to serve

1 Preheat the oven to 200°C/400°F/Gas Mark 6. Wash and dry the apples. Make a shallow cut through the skin around the middle of each apple – this will help the apples to cook through.

2 Core the apples, brush the centres with the lemon juice to prevent browning and stand in a shallow ovenproof dish.

3 In a bowl, mix together the blackberries, almonds, allspice, lemon rind and sugar. Using a teaspoon, spoon the mixture into the centre of each apple.

4 Pour the port into the dish, add the cinnamon stick and bake the apples in the oven for 35–40 minutes or until tender and soft. Drain the cooking juices into a pan and keep the apples warm.

5 Discard the cinnamon and add the cornflour (cornstarch) mixture to the cooking juices. Heat, stirring, until thickened.

6 Heat the custard until piping hot. Pour the sauce over the apples and serve with the custard.

VARIATION

Use raspberries instead of blackberries and, if you prefer, replace the port with unsweetened orange juice.

White Lace Crêpes with Oriental Fruits

Serves 4 • CALORIES PER SERVING: 170 • FAT CONTENT PER SERVING: 1.5 G

INGREDIENTS

3 medium egg whites
4 tbsp cornflour (cornstarch)
3 tbsp cold water
1 tsp vegetable oil

FRUIT FILLING:
350 g/12 oz fresh lychees
1/4 Galia melon
175 g/6 oz seedless green grapes
1 cm/1/2 inch piece root (fresh) ginger
2 pieces stem ginger in syrup
2 tbsp ginger wine or dry sherry

1 To make the fruit filling, peel the lychees and remove the stones. Place the lychees in a bowl. Scoop out the seeds from the melon and remove the skin. Cut the melon flesh into small pieces and place in the bowl.

2 Wash and dry the grapes, remove the stalks and add to the bowl. Peel the ginger and cut into thin shreds or grate finely. Drain the stem ginger pieces, reserving the syrup, and chop the ginger pieces quite finely.

3 Mix the gingers into the bowl along with the ginger wine or sherry and the reserved stem ginger syrup. Cover and set aside.

4 Meanwhile, prepare the crêpes. In a small jug, mix together the egg whites, cornflour (cornstarch) and cold water until very smooth.

5 Brush a small non-stick crêpe pan with oil and heat until hot. Drizzle the surface of the pan with a quarter of the cornflour (cornstarch) mixture to give a lacy effect. Cook for a few seconds until set, then carefully lift out and transfer to absorbent kitchen paper to drain. Set aside and keep warm. Repeat with the remaining mixture to make 4 crêpes in total.

6 To serve, place a crêpe on each serving plate and top with the fruit filling. Fold over the pancake and serve hot.

Fruit Loaf with Strawberry & Apple Spread

Serves 8 • CALORIES PER SERVING: 360 • FAT CONTENT PER SERVING: 2.8 G

INGREDIENTS

175 g/6 oz porridge oats (oatmeal)
100 g/3½ oz light muscovado sugar
1 tsp ground cinnamon
125 g/4½ oz sultanas
175 g/6 oz seedless raisins
2 tbsp malt extract
300 ml/½ pint/1¼ cups unsweetened apple juice
175 g/6 oz self-raising wholemeal (whole wheat) flour
1½ tsp baking powder
strawberries and apple wedges, to serve

FRUIT SPREAD:
225 g/8 oz strawberries, washed and hulled
2 eating (dessert) apples, cored, chopped and mixed with 1 tbsp lemon juice to prevent browning
300 ml/½ pint/1¼ cups unsweetened apple juice

1 Preheat the oven to 180°C/350°F/Gas Mark 4. Grease and line a 900 g/2 lb loaf tin (pan). Place the porridge oats (oatmeal), sugar, cinnamon, sultanas, raisins and malt extract in a bowl. Pour in the apple juice, stir well and leave to soak for 30 minutes.

2 Sift in the flour and baking powder, adding any husks that remain in the sieve, and fold in using a metal spoon. Spoon the mixture into the tin (pan) and bake for 1½ hours until firm or until a skewer inserted into the centre comes out clean. Cool for 10 minutes, then turn on to a rack and cool completely.

3 To make the fruit spread, place the strawberries and apples in a pan and pour in the apple juice. Bring to the boil, cover and simmer for 30 minutes. Beat the sauce well and spoon into a clean, warmed jar. Leave to cool, then seal and label.

4 Serve the loaf with 1–2 tbsp of the fruit spread and an assortment of apples and strawberries.

Banana & Lime Cake

Serves 10 • CALORIES PER SERVING: 360 • FAT CONTENT PER SERVING: 2.8 G

INGREDIENTS

300 g/10½ oz plain (all-purpose) flour
1 tsp salt
1½ tsp baking powder
175 g/6 oz light muscovado sugar
1 tsp lime rind, grated
1 medium egg, beaten
1 medium banana, mashed with 1 tbsp lime juice
150 ml/5 fl oz/⅔ cup low-fat natural fromage frais (unsweetened yogurt)
115 g/4 oz sultanas
banana chips and finely grated lime rind, to decorate

TOPPING:
115 g/4 oz icing (confectioner's) sugar
1–2 tsp lime juice
½ tsp lime rind, finely grated

1 Preheat the oven to 180°C/350°F/Gas Mark 4. Grease and line a deep 18 cm/7 inch round cake tin (pan) with baking parchment. Sift the flour, salt and baking powder into a bowl and stir in the sugar and lime rind.

2 Make a well in the centre of the dry ingredients and add the egg, banana, fromage frais (yogurt) and sultanas. Mix well until incorporated.

3 Spoon the mixture into the tin and smooth the surface. Bake for 40–45 minutes until firm to the touch or until a skewer inserted in the centre comes out clean. Leave to cool for 10 minutes, then turn out on to a wire rack.

4 For the topping, sift the icing (confectioner's) sugar into a bowl and mix with the lime juice to form a soft, but not too runny, icing. Stir in the lime rind. Drizzle the icing over the cake, letting it run down the sides.

5 Decorate with banana chips and lime rind. Let stand for 15 minutes so that the icing sets.

VARIATION

Replace the lime rind and juice with orange and the sultanas with chopped apricots.

1

2

3

Crispy Sugar-topped Blackberry & Apple Cake

Serves 10 • Calories per serving: 230 • Fat content per serving: 1.5 g

INGREDIENTS

350 g/12 oz cooking apples
3 tbsp lemon juice
300 g/10½ oz self-raising wholemeal (whole wheat) flour
½ tsp baking powder
1 tsp ground cinnamon, plus extra for dusting
175 g/6 oz prepared blackberries, thawed if frozen, plus extra to decorate
175 g/6 oz light muscovado sugar
1 medium egg, beaten
200 ml/7 fl oz/¾ cup low-fat natural fromage frais (unsweetened yogurt)
60 g/2 oz white or brown sugar cubes, lightly crushed
sliced eating (dessert) apple, to decorate

1 Preheat the oven to 190°C/375°F/Gas Mark 5. Grease and line a 900 g/2 lb loaf tin (pan). Core, peel and dice the apples. Place them in a pan with the lemon juice, bring to the boil, cover and simmer for 10 minutes until soft. Beat well and let cool.

2 Sift the flour, baking powder and 1 tsp cinnamon into a bowl, adding any husks that remain in the sieve. Stir in 115 g/4 oz blackberries and the sugar.

3 Make a well in the centre of the ingredients and add the egg, fromage frais (yogurt) and cooled apple purée. Mix well. Spoon the mixture into the prepared loaf tin (pan) and smooth over the top.

4 Sprinkle with the remaining blackberries, pressing them down into the cake mixture, and top with the crushed sugar lumps. Bake for 40–45 minutes. Leave to cool in the tin (pan).

5 Remove the cake from the tin and peel away the lining paper. Serve dusted with cinnamon and decorated with extra fruit.

Rich Fruit Cake

Serves 12 • Calories per serving: 315 • Fat content per serving: 3 g

INGREDIENTS

175 g/6 oz unsweetened pitted dates
115 g/4 oz no-need-to-soak dried prunes
200 ml/7 fl oz/¾ cup unsweetened orange juice
2 tbsp treacle (molasses)
1 tsp finely grated lemon rind
1 tsp finely grated orange rind
225 g/8 oz self-raising wholemeal (whole wheat) flour
1 tsp mixed spice
115 g/4 oz seedless raisins
115 g/4 oz golden sultanas
115 g/4 oz currants
115 g/4 oz dried cranberries
3 large eggs, separated
icing (confectioner's) sugar, to dust

TO DECORATE:
1 tbsp apricot jam, softened,
175 g/6 oz sugarpaste
strips of orange rind
strips of lemon rind

1 Preheat the oven to 170°C/325°F/Gas Mark 3. Grease and line a deep 20.5 cm/8 inch round cake tin (pan). Chop the dates and prunes and place in a pan. Pour over the orange juice and bring to the boil. Simmer for 10 minutes until very soft. Remove the pan from the heat and beat the fruit mixture until puréed. Stir in the treacle (molasses) and citrus rinds. Let cool.

2 Sift the flour and mixed spice into a bowl, adding any husks that remain in the sieve. Mix in the dried fruits and make a well in the centre.

3 When the date and prune mixture is cool, whisk in the egg yolks. In a separate bowl, whisk the egg whites until stiff. Spoon the fruit and egg yolk mixture into the dry ingredients and mix.

4 Fold in the egg whites using a metal spoon. Transfer to the tin (pan) and bake for 1½ hours. Leave to cool in the tin (pan).

5 Remove the cake from the tin (pan) and brush the top with jam. Dust the work surface with icing (confectioner's) sugar and roll out the sugarpaste thinly. Lay the sugarpaste over the top of the cake and trim the edges. Decorate.

Carrot & Ginger Cake

Serves 10 • CALORIES PER SERVING: 300 • FAT CONTENT PER SERVING: 10 G

INGREDIENTS

225 g/8 oz plain (all-purpose) flour
1 tsp baking powder
1 tsp bicarbonate of soda
2 tsp ground ginger
1/2 tsp salt
175 g/6 oz light muscovado sugar
225 g/8 oz carrots, grated
2 pieces stem ginger in syrup, drained and chopped
25 g/1 oz root (fresh) ginger, grated
60 g/2 oz seedless raisins
2 medium eggs, beaten
3 tbsp corn oil
juice of 1 medium orange

FROSTING:
225 g/8 oz low-fat soft cheese
4 tbsp icing (confectioner's) sugar
1 tsp vanilla essence (extract)

TO DECORATE:
grated carrot
stem (fresh) ginger
ground ginger

1 Preheat the oven to 180°C/350°F/Gas Mark 4. Grease and line a 20.5 cm/8 inch round cake tin (pan).

2 Sift the flour, baking powder, bicarbonate of soda, ground ginger and salt into a bowl. Stir in the sugar, carrots, stem ginger, root (fresh) ginger and raisins. Make a well in the centre of the dry ingredients.

3 Beat together the eggs, oil and orange juice, then pour into the centre of the well. Combine the ingredients together.

4 Spoon the mixture into the tin and smooth the surface. Bake in the oven for 1–1 1/4 hours until firm to the touch, or until a skewer inserted into the centre comes out clean. Cool in the tin (pan).

5 To make the frosting, place the soft cheese in a bowl and beat to soften. Sift in the icing (confectioner's) sugar and add the vanilla essence (extract). Stir well to mix.

6 Remove the cake from the tin (pan) and smooth the frosting over the top. Decorate and serve.

2

3

5

Strawberry Roulade

Serves 8 • CALORIES PER SERVING: 185 • FAT CONTENT PER SERVING: 4 G

INGREDIENTS

3 large eggs
115 g/4 oz caster (superfine) sugar
115 g/4 oz plain (all-purpose) flour
1 tbsp hot water

FILLING:
200 ml/7 fl oz/3/4 cup low-fat natural fromage frais (unsweetened yogurt)
1 tsp almond essence (extract)
225 g/8 oz small strawberries

15 g/1/2 oz toasted almonds, flaked (slivered)
1 tsp icing (confectioner's) sugar

1 Preheat the oven to 220°C/425°F/Gas Mark 7. Line a 35 x 25 cm/14 x 10 inch Swiss roll tin (pan) with parchment. Place the eggs in a bowl with the caster (superfine) sugar. Place the bowl over a pan of hot water and whisk until pale and thick.

2 Remove the bowl from the pan. Sift in the flour and fold into the eggs with the hot water. Pour the mixture into the tin (pan) and bake for 8–10 minutes, until golden and set.

3 Transfer the mixture to a sheet of parchment. Peel off the lining paper and roll up the sponge along with the parchment. Wrap in a tea towel (dish towel) and let cool.

4 To make the filling, mix together the fromage frais (yogurt) and almond essence (extract). Reserving a few strawberries for decoration, wash, hull and slice the rest. Leave the filling mixture to chill until ready to assemble.

5 Unroll the sponge, spread the fromage frais (yogurt) mixture over the sponge and sprinkle with the strawberries. Roll the sponge up again. Sprinkle with the almonds and lightly dust with icing (confectioner's) sugar. Decorate with the reserved strawberries.

VARIATION

Serve the roulade with a fruit purée, sweetened with a little sugar.

Fruity Muffins

Makes 10 • CALORIES PER SERVING: 180 • FAT CONTENT PER SERVING: 1.5 G

INGREDIENTS

225 g/8 oz self-raising wholemeal (whole wheat) flour
2 tsp baking powder
25 g/1 oz light muscovado sugar
100 g/3 1/2 oz no-need-to-soak dried apricots, chopped finely
1 medium banana, mashed with 1 tbsp orange juice
1 tsp orange rind, grated finely
300 ml/1/2 pint/1 1/4 cups skimmed milk
1 medium egg, beaten
3 tbsp corn oil
2 tbsp porridge oats (oatmeal)
fruit spread, honey or maple syrup, to serve

1 Preheat the oven to 200°C/400°F/Gas Mark 6. Place 10 paper muffin cases in a deep patty tin (pan).

2 Sift the flour and baking powder into a bowl, adding any husks that remain in the sieve. Stir in the sugar and apricots.

3 Make a well in the centre of the dry ingredients and add the banana, orange rind, milk, beaten egg and oil. Mix to form a thick batter. Divide the batter evenly among the 10 paper cases.

4 Sprinkle with a few porridge oats (oatmeal) and bake for 25–30 minutes until well risen and firm to the touch, or until a skewer inserted into the centre comes out clean. Transfer to a wire rack to cool slightly.

5 Serve the muffins warm with a little fruit spread, honey or maple syrup.

VARIATION

If you like dried figs, they make a deliciously crunchy alternative to the apricots; they also go very well with the flavour of orange. Other no-need-to-soak dried fruits, chopped up finely, can be used as well. Store these muffins in an airtight container for 3-4 days. They also freeze well in sealed bags or in freezer containers for up to 3 months.

2

3

4

Chocolate Brownies

Makes 12 • CALORIES PER SERVING: 300 • FAT CONTENT PER SERVING: 4.5 G

INGREDIENTS

60 g/2 oz unsweetened pitted dates, chopped
60 g/2 oz no-need-to-soak dried prunes, chopped
6 tbsp unsweetened apple juice
4 medium eggs, beaten
300 g/10½ oz dark muscovado sugar
1 tsp vanilla essence (extract)
4 tbsp low-fat drinking chocolate powder
2 tbsp cocoa powder
175 g/6 oz plain (all-purpose) flour
60 g/2 oz dark chocolate chips

ICING:
115 g/4 oz icing (confectioner's) sugar
1–2 tsp water
1 tsp vanilla essence (extract)

1 Preheat the oven to 180°C/350°F/Gas Mark 4. Grease and line a 18 x 28 cm/7 x 11 inch cake tin (pan) with parchment. Place the dates and prunes in a small pan and add the apple juice. Bring to the boil, cover and simmer for 10 minutes until soft. Beat to form a smooth paste, then set aside to cool.

2 Place the cooled fruit in a mixing bowl and stir in the eggs, sugar and vanilla essence. Sift in 4 tbsp drinking chocolate, the cocoa and the flour, and fold in along with the chocolate chips until well incorporated.

3 Spoon the mixture into the prepared tin (pan) and smooth over the top. Bake for 25–30 minutes until firm to the touch or until a skewer inserted into the centre comes out clean. Cut into 12 bars and leave to cool in the tin (pan) for 10 minutes. Transfer to a wire rack to cool completely.

4 To make the icing, sift the sugar into a bowl and mix with enough water and the vanilla essence (extract) to form a soft, but not too runny, icing.

5 Drizzle the icing over the chocolate brownies and allow to set. Dust with extra chocolate powder before serving.

Cheese & Chive Scones

Makes 10 • CALORIES PER SERVING: 120 • FAT CONTENT PER SERVING: 2.8 G

INGREDIENTS

250 g/9 oz self-raising flour
1 tsp powdered mustard
1/2 tsp cayenne pepper
1/2 tsp salt
100 g/3 1/2 oz low-fat soft cheese with added herbs
2 tbsp fresh snipped chives, plus extra to garnish
100 ml/3 1/2 fl oz and 2 tbsp skimmed milk
60 g/2 oz reduced-fat Cheddar cheese, grated
low-fat soft cheese, to serve

1 Preheat the oven to 200°C/400°F/Gas Mark 6. Sift the flour, mustard, cayenne and salt into a mixing bowl.

2 Add the soft cheese to the mixture and mix together until well incorporated. Stir in the snipped chives.

3 Make a well in the centre of the ingredients and gradually pour in 100 ml/3½ fl oz milk, stirring as you pour, until the mixture forms a soft dough.

4 Turn the dough on to a floured surface and knead lightly. Roll out until 2 cm/¾ inch thick and use a 5 cm/2 inch plain pastry cutter to stamp out as many rounds as you can. Transfer the rounds to a baking sheet (cookie sheet).

5 Re-knead the dough trimmings together and roll out again. Stamp out more rounds – you should be able to make 10 scones in total.

6 Brush the scones with the remaining milk and sprinkle with the grated cheese. Bake in the oven for 15–20 minutes until risen and golden. Transfer to a wire rack to cool. Serve warm with low-fat soft cheese, garnished with freshly snipped chives.

VARIATION

For sweet scones, omit the mustard, cayenne pepper, chives and grated cheese and add 75g/3 oz currants or sultanas and 25 g/1 oz sugar, and use plain low-fat soft cheese.

Savoury Tomato & (Bell) Pepper Bread

Serves 8 • CALORIES PER SERVING: 250 • FAT CONTENT PER SERVING: 3 G

INGREDIENTS

1 small red (bell) pepper
1 small green (bell) pepper
1 small yellow (bell) pepper
60 g/2 oz dry-pack sun-dried tomatoes
50 ml/2 fl oz/$^{1}/_{4}$ cup boiling water
2 tsp dried yeast
1 tsp caster (superfine) sugar
150 ml/5 fl oz/$^{2}/_{3}$ cup tepid water
450 g/1 lb/4 cups strong white bread flour
2 tsp dried rosemary
2 tbsp tomato purée (paste)
150 ml/5 fl oz/$^{2}/_{3}$ cup low-fat natural fromage frais (unsweetened yogurt)
1 tbsp coarse salt
1 tbsp olive oil

1 Preheat the oven to 220°C/425°F/Gas Mark 7 and the grill (broiler) to hot. Halve and deseed the (bell) peppers, arrange on the rack and cook until the skin is charred. Cool for 10 minutes, peel off the skin and chop the flesh.

2 Slice the tomatoes into strips and place in a bowl. Pour over the boiling water and set aside to soak.

3 Place the yeast and sugar in a small jug, pour over the tepid water and leave for 10–15 minutes until frothy. Sift the flour into a bowl and add 1 tsp dried rosemary. Make a well in the centre and pour in the yeast mixture. Add the tomato purée (paste), the tomatoes and soaking liquid, the (bell) peppers, fromage frais (yogurt) and half the salt. Mix together to form a soft dough.

4 Turn the dough out on to a floured surface and knead for 3–4 minutes until smooth and elastic. Place in a floured bowl, cover and leave in a warm room for about 40 minutes until doubled in size. Knead again and place in a greased 23 cm/9 inch round spring-clip cake tin (pan). Make 'dimples' in the surface. Cover for 30 minutes.

5 Brush with oil and sprinkle with rosemary and salt. Bake for 35–40 minutes, cool for 10 minutes and release from the tin (pan). Leave to cool.

Index

Index compiled by Hilary Bird.